Longman Proficiency Skills
Teacher's Guide

Roy Kingsbury and Mary Spratt

Longman

LONGMAN GROUP UK LIMITED
Longman House, Burnt Mill, Harlow,
Essex, CM20 2JE, England
and Associated Companies throughout the world.

First published 1985
Fifth impression 1989

Set in Monophoto Plantin medium
Produced by Longman Group (FE) Ltd
Printed in Hong Kong

Authors' Acknowledgements

Our sincere thanks to Paul Murphy and Jo
Tierney at the British Institute, Lisbon, and to
Mrs Pat Hughes of the Hinton School of
English, Bournemouth, for piloting and
commenting on these materials. Also, our
thanks to Hara Garoufalia-Middle for her
comments.

ISBN 0 582 55939 1

Course Syllabus

Cambridge Proficiency Paper	Contents of Units (*S* = Skills; *G* = Grammar; *V* = Vocabulary)
Paper 1: Reading Comprehension	**1 Heredity or Environment?** *S* Reading Skills: Skimming, Scanning, Reading for detail, Guessing meaning from context, Inference. *G* Inversion constructions with *Not only . . . but also . . ., Never . . ., Seldom . . ., No sooner . . . than . . ., Scarcely/Hardly . . . when/before . . ., Nowhere . . .*, etc.
Paper 2: Composition	**2 Generations** *S* Discursive Composition: Planning and Writing. *G* Verb + noun/pronoun/possessive adj. + gerund. *V* Expressions for listing, exemplifying, rephrasing and concluding. Joining words *though, whereas, despite, moreover, besides*, etc.
Paper 3: Use of English	**3 Mysteries and Theories** *S* Summary writing, and completing blanks in passages. *G* The use or absence of Definite Article *the* with names of planets, continents, countries, mountains, lakes, rivers, festivals and seasons, people's names, etc.
Paper 4: Listening Comprehension	**4 Crime and Punishment** *S* Listening to non-standard English accents. Interpreting graphs, etc. Predicting. *G* Adverb and adjective constructions: *bigger and bigger, more and more slowly; the sooner, the better; sad as/though it is . . ., so sharp/sharply . . . that . . .* *V* Adverb–adjective collocations: *absolutely amazed, bitterly disappointed*, etc.
Paper 5: Interview	**5 Consumer Society** *S* Talking about a photo, and Dealing with passages. *G* Relative pronouns *which, who* and *that*. Participle *-ing* constructions: *Being a busy housewife . . ., Not having . . ., While waiting . . ., On plugging in . . .*, etc. *V* Compound nouns: *a carving knife, a coffee grinder, a wristwatch, an air hostess*, etc.

6 Science and Science Fiction

S   Answering multiple-choice questions, and building vocabulary.

G   Some revision of Present Perfect, Simple Past and Past Perfect tenses.

V   Related verbs e.g. *sink, tumble, topple, capsize, slump*.
Vocabulary areas and collocation.

7 The Energy Debate

S   'Directed Writing' Composition – newspaper article, letter, etc.: Style.

G   Modal verbs and noun replacements e.g. *obligation, necessity, possibility*, etc.
Modals with *there* e.g. *There must be . . ., There could have been . . .*, etc.
Infinitive and gerund modal forms: *to have to, having been able to*, etc.

8 The Technological Revolution

S   Answering questions on a passage and explaining phrases.

G   Passive constructions: revision plus *I didn't hear my name called./I want to be left alone./ There's a lot to be done./He was nowhere to be found.* etc.

V   Nouns from phrasal verbs e.g. *onset, outbreak, upkeep, drawback*, etc.

9 Personal Experiences

S   Multiple-choice questions on Listening: reading, predicting, answering.

G   Reported Speech constructions: *Speaking at the meeting . . ., Asked about the possibility . . . .*

V   Formal and informal reporting verbs.
Verbs when reporting: *congratulate, promise*, etc.; *whisper, snap, bawl*, etc.

10 Mind over Matter

S   Talking about a photo, Dealing with passages, and Discussion.

G   Variations on *if*-clauses: *Do this, and you'll get . . .; Should you be interested . . .; Were it not for/But for the rain . . .; Had I been there . . .;* etc.

V   Related nouns and verbs: *a 'record/to re'cord; ad'vice/to ad'vise*; etc.

11 Television, Films and Photography

S   Recognising author's style, purpose and attitude, and connotations (positive, negative, neutral) e.g. *edit/scribble/write*.
Exam Guidance and Advice for Paper 1
Reading Comprehension.

12 People, Places, Experiences, Events

S   Descriptive and Narrative Compositions: Planning and Writing.
Analysing a description, choosing appropriate vocabulary, and structuring a description.

Exam Guidance and Advice for Paper 2
Composition.

13 Preservation and Conservation

S   Completing blanks in sentences and dialogues.
More summary writing.

Exam Guidance and Advice for Paper 3
Use of English.

14 Leisure and Health

S   Listening for speakers' moods, feelings and attitudes.
Register in speech: formal and informal, and professional/occupational.

Exam Guidance and Advice for Paper 4
Listening Comprehension.

15 Aspects of Education

S   Talking about a photo, Dealing with passages, and Participating in structured communication exercises.

Exam Guidance and Advice for Paper 5
Interview.

General introduction

Background information

1 Who the course is for

Longman Proficiency Skills is designed for students preparing specifically for the Cambridge Certificate of Proficiency in English Examination. To follow this course students don't need to have taken the Cambridge First Certificate Examination, but they do need to be well beyond First Certificate level and preferably to have already followed a post-First Certificate course. Passing the Cambridge Proficiency Examination requires an extremely good command of English on both the written and the spoken levels.

2 The Cambridge Proficiency Examination

The Cambridge Proficiency Examination is designed as follows:

PAPER 1 Reading Comprehension	Section A – 25 multiple-choice vocabulary questions Section B – 15 multiple-choice questions on two or three reading passages
PAPER 2 Composition	A choice of two out of four compositions (or five if students study the optional literature component★)

PAPER 3
Use of English
	Section A – blank-filling, transformation and completion
	   grammar exercises
	Section B – open-ended reading comprehension questions
	   on a text and summary writing

PAPER 4 Listening Comprehension	Questions or tasks (e.g. chart-filling) on various pieces of recorded language
PAPER 5 Interview	An oral interview of three parts with an examiner Part 1 – talking about a photo Part 2 – commenting on a short passage Part 3 – structured communication exercise

★ Students are given the option of reading one or more of a number of set books. If they choose to do this, they can then answer the literature composition in Paper 2 and will also have an opportunity to talk about the book(s) in the Interview if they wish.

3 The level of the Cambridge Proficiency Examination

To pass the Cambridge Proficiency Examination students must have a near fluent command of both the spoken and written language. For this reason students cannot simply rely on a coursebook or language classes to help them through the exam. They must also do as much reading, speaking, listening to and writing of English outside the classroom as possible.

4 Design criteria for the course

Longman Proficiency Skills was constructed to give practice in two kinds of skills – language skills and examination skills.

Content of the course

1 Materials

The course consists of:

A Coursebook
Teacher's Guide
A set of Cassettes

2 The Coursebook

The Coursebook consists of:

15 Units
A Proficiency Practice Exam
Listening Comprehension texts (transcripts of all the Listening Comprehension
materials used in the Coursebook *except* the end-of-Unit tests and Practice Exam)

3 The Teacher's Guide

The Teacher's Guide consists of:

A General Introduction
Unit-by-Unit teaching notes including transcripts of the Listening tests and Practice
Exam Listening Comprehension Paper 4
Answers to the Practice Exam and suggested marking schemes

Design of the Coursebook

1 A cyclical approach

Longman Proficiency Skills has a cyclical progression which focuses on each
Proficiency Paper three times as follows:

Reading Comprehension:	Units 1, 6, 11
Composition:	Units 2, 7, 12
Use of English:	Units 3, 8, 13
Listening Comprehension:	Units 4, 9, 14
Interview:	Units 5, 10, 15

This cyclical progression allows for an accumulative and graded presentation of
materials, language and skills within each Paper. It is therefore possible to start the
book not only at the beginning but also at the beginning of any of the separate
Paper cycles.

2 Teaching and testing

We believe that students preparing for the Proficiency Examination need to
improve their language and language skills and also to master the test techniques
required by the exam. For this reason the *Longman Proficiency Skills* Coursebook
materials are of two types: teaching materials and testing materials. These are
distributed throughout the Coursebook as follows:

1 Each Unit contains teaching materials plus a test at the end of the Unit.
2 Units 11–15 each contain teaching materials plus Exam Guidance in the form of
  'worked' test material, as well as Exam Advice.
3 Following the 15 Units there is a complete Proficiency Practice Exam.

3 Course syllabus

Three concerns have influenced the syllabus of *Longman Proficiency Skills:*

1 the requirements of the Proficiency Examination;
2 students' needs regarding language and language skills;
3 the need for students to be interested and motivated to study and learn well.

The requirements of the Proficiency Examination: The Cambridge Proficiency Examination does not work to a published syllabus. Nevertheless, particular structures, vocabulary areas, topics, language skills and examination or testing techniques constantly occur in the exams and the wide range of materials in the Coursebook is designed to cater for these.

Students' needs regarding language and language skills: At this level students from whatever language background reveal common weaknesses e.g. in composition writing, in the mastery of degrees of formality in language, in the use of exact and detailed vocabulary and in the use of particular grammatical structures. The Coursebook is designed to cater for these.

The need for students to be interested and motivated to study and learn well: Few students can continue to study and learn to their full capacity just with the motivation of aiming towards an examination. Students need to enjoy learning, be interested in it and see its relevance to themselves as human beings. This is one reason why the Coursebook has deliberately included a wide range of topics, texts and listening comprehension pieces of general interest, as well as a wide variety of classroom activities. The Coursebook also aims to involve the students as much as possible in the processes of learning so as to interest and motivate them. For this reason you will see that much information about the exam, its techniques and ways of approaching them have been included in the Coursebook and that this information has been given in a conversational and direct style.

The design and content of each Unit

There is some variety in the design and content of each Unit in response to the differing demands of each of the Proficiency Papers. However, within this variety certain elements recur in each Unit. These are:

– a warm-up or lead-in activity
– a focus on particular skills required for the Proficiency Paper under study
– a Grammar section
– Homework
– a test

Warm-up or lead-in activities: These are intended, as their name suggests, simply to lead students into the topic of a Unit and to motivate them to think about it. In this way it is hoped that they won't approach a text, listening comprehension piece or photo cold or without some interest in finding out more from it.

A focus on particular skills: These vary greatly in the Units as the needs of students and the demands of the exam are many.

Grammar: At this level students should have mastered the basic grammatical patterns of the language. They now need to extend and refine these patterns, particularly to achieve greater mastery of complex sentences, and also to gain greater accuracy in handling those grammatical structures which are most appropriate to a particular situation or style. In Units 1–10 one particular grammar point is given special focus in each Unit. In Units 11–15 the study of grammar is subsumed in the exam guidance and advice and takes on more the nature of revision and remedial work.

Homework: We have included homework in every Unit not just because we see it as a useful consolidation of classwork but also in recognition of the difficulty of the Proficiency Exam, which can only be overcome by ever-increasing exposure to the language. Students on a Proficiency Course must do homework to give them further contact with and practice in the language, and they need to do it within the recommended time to gain practice in timing.

End-of-Unit test: The tests at the end of each Unit are included so that from early on in the course students have a clear idea of the types of exercise and level of difficulty they will meet in the exam, and also to begin to master exam techniques and get used to working within required time limits. The time limits given in each test are all accurate reflections of the times set in the Proficiency Exam, and it is therefore important for students to work strictly within these limits. The tests do not constitute complete practice Exam Papers although they do grow longer and fuller as the Coursebook progresses. It is only in the Proficiency Practice Exam that there is an example of a full 'mock' Proficiency Exam. Although this exam is placed at the end of the book, teachers may well wish to show it to their students early on in the course so as to acquaint them with the content of the exam. We recommend that students do the tests in class under exam-like conditions and in the specified time limit. A marking scheme for each test is provided at the end of each Teaching Notes Unit.

N.B. There are no tests as such at the end of the Paper 5 Interview Units because it would be very difficult for most teachers to administer such tests in their normal working conditions. Interview materials are however provided to be used in class or to be done as a test by those teachers who can organise this.

Recorded material: The tapes contain all the listening material for each Unit, end-of-Unit tests where appropriate and the Listening Comprehension material required for Paper 4 of the Proficiency Practice Exam. The recordings are not authentic speech but they have been recorded to sound as natural as possible and contain a variety of 'non-standard' accents. Each Listening Comprehension piece is only given once on the tapes (with the exception of the Practice Exam materials). If students need to hear a piece again you will have to rewind the tape to the beginning of the piece and play it again.

Range of activities: While every Unit aims to teach and practise skills relevant to a specific Proficiency Paper, it will also include other activities. This is to maintain interest and also because it is not always natural or necessary to separate language skills.

Teaching notes

Each Unit in the Teaching notes contains:

– a detailed explanation of the aims of each Unit;
– a guide to each exercise or activity in the Unit which contains general information, suggested classroom treatment and answers;
– tapescripts for Listening Comprehension texts and tests;
– answers to tests and suggested marking schemes.

For most activities in the course the following information is given: the aim or aims of the activity, information on language points and language skills, information about the Proficiency Examination, information about the style of texts, suggested classroom treatment and answers, register, focus vocabulary, and any necessary cultural references.

Style: Information is given about the style of each text not only because style is becoming an ever more important factor in the Cambridge exam but also because recognition of different styles forms an important part of an advanced command of a language. The *Longman Dictionary of Contemporary English* defines style as 'a type of choice of words, especially which marks out the speaker or writer as different from others' *or* 'a general manner or way of doing anything which is typical or representative of a person or group, time in history, etc.' You will see that in accordance with this, texts are labelled as objective, dramatic, colourful, intimate, biased, etc.

Register: This is a linguistic term which is used to mean two different things. Firstly, it can refer to how formal a piece of language is e.g. very formal, casual, neutral, slang, etc. Secondly, it can refer to language which is typical of a particular profession or group of users e.g. legal register, advertising language, scientific language, business register, etc. Each of these fields is characterised by a regular use of particular words, styles and grammatical structures. Students at Proficiency level need to be able to recognise register in both its meanings and produce appropriately differing levels of formality in their own written and spoken language.

Focus vocabulary: This is vocabulary which students are intended to be able to recognise and use by the end of an activity. It may or may not represent all the unknown vocabulary contained in a text. Students should be discouraged from wanting to know the meaning of every single vocabulary item in a text as this slows down their comprehension, is not essential to their general comprehension and detracts from the pleasure of reading.
N.B. The explanations of the meanings of words which are given in the Teaching notes are only of those meanings which explain the word as used in the particular text. Students are advised to have a dictionary available when working with the Coursebook and for any work in English done outside the classroom.

Cultural information: This is provided for some texts which contain cultural references which need to be understood for comprehension of the text as a whole.

Classroom treatment

Under this heading suggestions are made as to how activities might be handled in class. The Coursebook also contains many suggestions of this kind.

Answers

Answers are provided in the Teaching notes to all the exercises and tasks in the Coursebook except those which might be described as 'open-ended', where only 'Suggested' or 'Possible' answers are given.

Classroom approaches

1 General

We believe that learning occurs most in interested and participating students in a relaxed yet challenging classroom atmosphere in which students can try out different learning strategies. For this reason the Coursebook contains individual, pair and group work, explanations, exercises, guided work and opportunities for free unstructured uses of language. The teacher in this context becomes not so much an information-giver as an organiser, animator, advisor and corrector.

2   The use of English in the classroom

English should be the only language used in the Proficiency classroom unless the teacher asks students to give the meaning of a particularly tricky word in the mother tongue just to check comprehension. If students are not used to only speaking English, they may do so unwillingly or only intermittently at first, particularly in pair and group work. The passage of time and the teacher's insistence on English will overcome this.

3   Individual, pair and group work

Individual work

Many of the activities in the Coursebook require students to work *individually* before checking their work with a partner or teacher. This is to ensure that *every* student in the class undertakes the activity concerned and not just one or a few students in the class.

Pair work

Many of the practice and checking activities in the Coursebook are recommended to be done in *pairs*. The reason for this is once again to involve students as much as possible in the use of the language. When pairs of students are busy using the language there is maximum practice. Pair work is also a good way of encouraging shyer students to contribute and it also gives teachers the opportunity to give their attention to weaker students.

Group work is often recommended in the Coursebook for discussions, summary work and reporting. This is because many heads can be better than one, i.e. the more opinions there are, the more you have to justify, think about and refine your own opinion. Group work is also another way of maximising student participation. For pair and group work to operate successfully students must be very clear about what they have to do and say. The Coursebook therefore carefully structures all these tasks, and further indications as to how to structure them are provided in the Classroom treatment sections of the Units in the Teaching notes.

During pair and group work the teacher must keep a close eye on students' work to make sure they have understood what they must do and also to provide help when it is needed. The teacher can therefore move around from pair to pair or group to group during these activities, or keep attentively to one side and not take any active part so as to encourage students to get on with the task set on their own. On some occasions it is useful to move from individual to pair to group work on the same task as this gives students an ever-increasing involvement in the task in hand, e.g.:

1   each student makes a decision
2   students discuss and justify their decisions in pairs
3   students discuss and justify their decisions in groups
4   students discuss and justify their decisions with the class as a whole.

This progression (known as 'pyramid work') is useful for many of the activities in the course.

4   The formation of pairs and groups

It is useful to vary the composition of pairs and groups across lessons so that students don't always work with the same people. In this way, all the class gets to know one another, students meet different personalities and ideas, and also the teacher can combine weak and strong students in different ways at different times as seems best.

5 Discussion work

The ideal discussion is clearly one in which as many students as possible participate and there is a minimum of teacher intervention. Discussions can be held either on the whole class level or in groups: the latter may have a spokesperson who then reports back to the whole class on the group's conclusions and thus provokes further discussion, this time on the class level. In either case it is advisable, before beginning a discussion, to give students a few minutes of silent reflection in which to collect together or jot down their thoughts on the topic of the discussion and also ask the teacher how to say in English any unknown vocabulary items they will need. In whole class discussions, once the discussion begins the teacher should say little, mainly acting as a chairperson who makes sure no particular person talks too much, that all important points are considered in the discussion and that everybody has an opportunity to put forward their point of view. Alternatively, the teacher could appoint a student to act as chairperson, in which case the teacher's role would become that of a noter-down of mistakes, as indicated below in *Correction procedures*. The teacher has a similar role to this if the discussion is done in groups.

N.B. Since it is much easier for students to talk if they can see one another, it is useful to have desks arranged as follows for class discussion work:

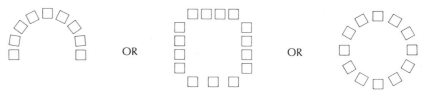

and similar but smaller arrangements for group discussions.

6 Correction procedures

Teachers may be anxious about how they can correct everyone's mistakes in pair and group work. The simple answer to this is that they can't! But more importantly, they shouldn't worry if they can't, partly because students will come to help and correct one another, particularly in well structured tasks, partly because even if uncorrected, students are gaining valuable fluency practice. Teachers moving round the class during group or pair work may choose to correct students or not to do so. If correcting means breaking the flow and rhythm of discussion, it is probably not worth doing at that precise moment. However, if a student is having obvious difficulty in expressing him/herself and is even anxious for help, then correction by the teacher can be useful. If, as the teacher wanders round the class listening to different pairs or groups, he/she notices mistakes but doesn't want to interrupt the activity, one solution is to note the mistakes down on a correction sheet and then, when the activity has finished, write the mistakes on the blackboard and ask students to correct them. A correction sheet could look as follows:

Pronunciation Mistakes	Grammatical Mistakes	Vocabulary Mistakes	Register Mistakes

7 Skills and tasks

You will notice in the Coursebook that reading and listening texts are followed by a wide range of different activities e.g. gist understanding, finding specific items of information, detailed comprehension, summary work, etc. Each of these activities helps to train a particular language skill and different texts will lend themselves much more to particular skills than certain other texts. For example, people rarely read a telephone directory to summarise its contents or read a job advertisement just to find out its general message. We therefore recommend you only to exploit the texts to the degree and in the way suggested in the Coursebook so as to allow students to train particular skills at any one time and also allow them to come to realise that there are different kinds of texts, whether written or spoken, which therefore require different kinds and levels of comprehension.

Teaching notes

Introduction

The following pages contain teaching notes on a Unit-by-Unit basis. For each Unit, th
following are provided where applicable:

Aims of the Unit

Notes for each exercise or activity with, as appropriate, notes on style, register and
focus vocabulary.

Tapescripts for Listening Comprehension texts.

Procedures for games, instructions, examples and suggested treatment.

Answers, Suggested answers or Possible answers to exercises.

End-of-Unit Test answer keys and suggested marking schemes, with tapescripts for
Listening Comprehension Tests.

N.B. In Tapescripts, an asterisk (*) indicates where you should pause the tape for
students to look at multiple-choice questions, graphs, etc.

UNIT 1 Heredity or Environment?

Aims of the Unit
1 To introduce students to five reading skills: skimming, scanning, reading for detail, guessing the meaning of words from context, and inferring.
2 Grammar: to review some Inversion Constructions and the use of certain tenses.
3 To expand students' knowledge of vocabulary connected to the topic of *Heredity and Environment*.

Coursebook pp 6–7

Exercise 1 The reason for getting students to note down their predictions is to make sure that they all think about the topic of the passage they are about to read, and all have predictions to compare with their partners'.

Exercise 2 The aim of this exercise is to train the reading skill of *skimming* (see further below under *Reading skills*, Coursebook p.8). It must therefore be done quickly and you could even set a time limit of 5 minutes. Don't let students run their fingers or a pencil along each line of the passage when doing this kind of reading, as to do so would mean that they were not skimming properly but reading for detail.

Style of text: descriptive, explanatory, factual

Register: neutral

Focus vocabulary
N.B. Do *not* teach this vocabulary as the meaning of these words must be worked out by students in Exercise **4**.
odds: the probability that something will or will not happen
painstaking: careful and thorough
to dwell: (*literary*) to live
fodder: things or people used for supplying a continuous demand
nurture: education, training or development
an inkling: a possible idea
marginally: slightly
a sibling: a brother or sister
startling: unexpected and slightly shocking

Cultural information
Jacob and Esau: biblical figures, twin sons. Jacob symbolised the pastoral nomad, and Esau the hunter and raider.
Romulus and Remus: twins, mythical founders of Rome, reared by a she-wolf
the workhouse: (in former times) a place for the poor to live when they had no employment, especially when old
the social services: welfare services provided by a government, especially those paid for (partly) by taxes, such as medical care, and the care of orphans, the poor, the elderly, the disabled, etc.

Possible answer The passage is about how sets of twins separated at birth have been reunited by a social worker and about a study carried out on similar sets of twins to establish the relative contributions of heredity and environment in humans.

Exercise 3   **Classroom treatment** Students should write the answers to these questions either individually or in pairs before the answers are checked with the class as a whole. This is to ensure that everyone has the opportunity to work on the passage.

Suggested answers

1 His connection is that it's his job to try to find and reunite such sets of twins.
2 He wouldn't have been, because these twins were raised together, and he is interested in twins raised apart.
3 Because during that period twins were more likely than at other times to be separated when adopted.
4 Because the law has changed, so now they can at least track down their original birth certificates.
5 Because it can be rather alarming to hear this kind of news unexpectedly from a stranger over the phone.
6 He considers his work to have been very successful as he thinks he has helped people to discover the truth about their own lives.

Exercise 4   In the exam students will almost certainly have to guess the meaning of words from
Vocabulary   context either to answer a question or to help them understand the gist of a passage. This is also an important skill for them to master for general reading in English as it allows them to read more fluently and confidently. Many students, however, need encouragement and help to see how the text can supply them with clues to the meaning of words.

The clues to the meaning of the words may come before or after the word in question, be close to that word or further away, and be grammatical and/or semantic clues.

The clues to the meaning of the words in this exercise are as follows:

odds: 240 to one against; longer odds; finding pairs . . . concerned
painstaking: patient detective work
dwelt: contrast with *hunter*; clue also provided by *in tents*
fodder: rich research fodder *for those who . . .*; *they are a select group*
nurture: *heredity or environment, nature versus* nurture; *identical heredity but different environments*
inkling: *knowing, or at least suspecting*
marginally: *easier; at least*
sibling: *lost* sibling
startling: he *gave up the telephone call* in favour of a *discreetly worded* letter; *if you're not expecting it*

Exercise 5   **Classroom treatment** Allow the students time to warm into the discussion topics.
Discussion   Don't expect them to do so immediately. Just stand back and let the students gently feel their way into them. It's important to conduct these discussions in small groups because at this stage of the course students don't know one another at all well, and are therefore often reluctant to talk in front of the whole class. Group work also provides them with a way of getting to know one another better. Select from the suggested discussions in response to what the students seem to be most interested in. The following could be used as extra discussion prompts if they are needed.

Discussion 1

What would you do/How would you react if someone rang you up and told you this kind of news? Would you be pleased/angry/anxious/curious, etc?
What kind of difference would such a revelation make to your life?

Why do you think the researchers did this research? What was their reason and motivation?
What effects do their work seem to have had?

Discussion 2

What does the research appear to have discovered? Do we know?
What findings do you imagine it could come up with?
Could such findings make any difference to methods of bringing up children, education or state intervention in either of these? Would this be a good thing?

Discussion 3

How can you explain that sometimes apparently average parents have brilliant children?
Why do some races seem to better at some things than others? Is this hereditary or conditioning from the environment?
From the point of view of character are you more like your mother or your father, or neither? And what about your brothers and sisters?

Coursebook pp 8–9

Reading Skills   The reading skills practised on these pages are particularly relevant to the Proficiency Exam with its variety of reading comprehension questions and task types. They are also important and useful general reading skills which, once mastered, allow students to read more fluently and efficiently. The different skills involve the following:

Skimming: reading superficially over a piece of writing to situate it and find out what it's about.

Scanning: finding the place in a piece of writing where a particular item of information is given and taking in that item of information. This kind of reading involves not reading in any detail at all large sections of the piece of writing.

Reading for detail: understanding the qualifying information contained in a piece of writing e.g. to recognise the meaning added by a particular adjectival clause, clause of concession, or adverb.

Guessing the meaning of words from context: see above Exercise 4 on page 8 of Coursebook.

Inference: drawing the meaning from something said i.e. beyond the literal meaning e.g. he never arrives at the meetings on time and my inference is that he feels they are useless.

Style of text: factual, descriptive, slightly sensational. N.B. Note the spelling of *program* in the text. This is the standard spelling for this word when it refers to computer programs.

Register: neutral

Focus vocabulary

N.B. Do *not* teach this vocabulary as the meaning of these words must be worked out by students in Exercise **4**.
calibre: the quality of something or someone
to launch: to cause to begin
a bonus: an additional payment beyond what is usual, necessary or expected

Cultural information

'O' levels: 'Ordinary' level exams of the General Certificate of Education (G.C.E.).
  Normally taken after 5 years of secondary school.
CSEs: 'Certificate of Secondary Education'. Exams which have a more practical,
  less academic bias than 'O' levels, taken in secondary school.

Classroom treatment

1 Read the explanation of the skill aloud with the class following.
2 Class discussion of the skill in which you might want to point out the information
  on the skills given above.
3 Students do the exercise individually and in writing.
4 Report back on answers.
5 As above with each of the skills.
6 Students could be asked whether they thought they already carry out these skills
  on English texts or with texts in their own language, and if so which skills they
  employ on what kind of text.

Answers

Exercise 1 It's about the rise to fame and success of a young boy through his work in
designing computer programs.

Exercise 2 1 £35,000 (line 2); 2 16 (line 7); 3 a Jaguar (line 10); 4 6 (line 20); 5 12 (line 25);
6 'Space Panic' (line 31); 7 £17,000 (line 35); 8 Image Software (line 32);
9 Liverpool (line 40); 10 bus driver (line 40)

Exercise 3 1 No, not yet.
2 Because he has such an exceptional job at so young an age.

Exercise 4 See *Focus vocabulary* above.

Exercise 5 1 Presumably not, because he read under the bedclothes.
2 Jealousy, because he's likely to earn seven times as much as his father.

Coursebook pp 10–11

Grammar Inversion Constructions are tested regularly in Section A of the Use of English
Exercise 1 Paper. These particular Inversion Constructions are somewhat formal and more a
feature of written than spoken language. Make sure students realise that inversion
only occurs after these words when they are placed at the beginning of a sentence.

Clasroom treatment

1 Read the explanation through with the class as a whole.
2 Ask students to write the answers indvidually.
3 Students check their answers in pairs.
4 Report back of answers to the whole class.

Answers

1 Rarely do people appreciate the full force of heredity.
2 No sooner had he left school than he started computer programming.
3 Not only has Eugene earned a fortune but he has also delighted his father.
4 Not until the twins have met for the first time will we know how they feel about
  each other./Not until they have met for the first time will we know how the
  twins feel about each other.
5 Never before has such research been carried out.
6 Seldom do you find reunited twins who do not get on well together.
7 Scarcely had Eugene Evans left school before he found a job in a computer
  software company.

8 Only when he started work did he realise how talented he was.

9 Hardly had they been reunited before/when they were deep in conversation about the past.

10 Nowhere will you find a school whose pupils get such good results.

Exercise 2
Tenses

The purpose of this exercise is to get students actively and consciously thinking about why particular tenses are used. While enabling them to answer Use of English type questions, it will also make them become critical and aware of their own use of tenses and sensitive to the shades of meaning of different tenses.

N.B. Some students may not be familiar with the names of the tenses in English – this is the opportunity to teach them.

Classroom treatment Allow students time to read through and reflect on the questions before answering them. Check at this stage that all the grammatical labels are understood. Encourage as much discussion on the answers as possible so that any doubts or misunderstandings the students may have become apparent and can therefore be dealt with.

Answers

1 The Simple Past tense is used in no. 2 because the actions referred to i.e. starting computer programming and leaving school, are actions that are complete and belong entirely to the past. By contrast, the Present Perfect tense is used in no. 3 because the action of delighting his father, although beginning in the past, is still true of now, i.e. it continues into the present.

2 Because the sentence contains a reference to present time. The action began in the past but it is still continuing.

3 Because the verb describes a permanent rather than a temporary present attitude.

4 Because Eugene is no longer realising how talented he is and only started work once in the past i.e. neither action is continued in the present.

5 Past Perfect and then Simple Past. The Past Perfect is used to show that this action happened before the other.

Homework exercise
Composition

Explain to students how vital it is for them to do homework and to get as much practice in composition writing as possible.

Make sure they include their composition plans in the homework they hand in to you, so that you can see whether their problems lie in planning or writing the composition.

Stress too that they keep to the recommended time limit which is the one they will have to work to in the exam.

Explain that correct timing is an important exam skill.

Test
Reading
Comprehension

1 Explain to students that the end-of-Unit tests are *not* of the same length as the Proficiency Exam Papers and that because of this they won't necessarily contain all the exercise types contained in a particular Paper. Explain that the time limit is, however, an accurate scale-down of the time they will be allowed in the Proficiency Exam.

2 We recommend you to get students to do the test in class under exam-like conditions and in the recommended time.

Answers

1 D; 2 C; 3 B; 4 B.

Suggested marking
scheme

2 marks for each correct answer.
Total possible score for whole test: 8 marks.

UNIT 2 Generations

PAPER 2: **COMPOSITION**

Aims of the Unit
1 To consolidate some of the reading skills introduced in Unit 1.
2 To introduce and work on composition planning.
3 To examine discursive composition writing.
4 To establish a procedure for composition writing.
5 To provide vocabulary and phrases for introducing or linking sentences.
6 Grammar: to review the pattern:
verb + noun/pronoun/possessive adjective + gerund.
7 To expand students' knowledge of vocabulary connected to the topic of
Generations.

Coursebook pp 12–13

Exercise 1 The purpose of asking students to think of a good headline for this article is to encourage them to read for gist.

Style of text: detailed, objective, undramatic, impersonal

Register: neutral

Focus vocabulary

a tramp: a person with no home or job, who wanders from place to place begging for food or money.
Cockney: a Londoner, especially one from the East End.

Cultural information

a special unit: a special school run by a local education authority to deal with 'problem children'.
glue sniffing: this is a growing addiction in the U.K. The consequences of sniffing glue can cause serious health problems.
a skinhead: a youth (usually a boy) in Britain with his hair cut very short. Skinheads have a reputation for being violent.
Cockney: this accent was originally a working class one from the East End of London. Its connotations are liveliness, quick-wit, sharp intelligence and also low class and defiance of middle-class values. These latter connotations are those relevant in the article.
to be in care: in England 'problem' teenagers are sometimes placed 'in care', i.e. sent to residential centres which they are only allowed to leave with the permission of the authorities. These centres provide education and sport as well as contact with social workers who try to help solve each resident's problems. Teenagers can be placed in care for varying amounts of time. Parents are allowed to see their children at special times only as visiting is strictly regulated.

Classroom treatment For the gist reading keep strictly to the time limit suggested so as to get students used to skimming texts when this is appropriate.

Answers

Gist: It's the details related by a mother of the chain of events which lead to her son being placed in care. (N.B. The wording of this gist can, of course, vary considerably, but not the content.)

Possible magazine headlines:
   – How I lost my son
   – A Mother's Tale
   – Where did I go wrong?

N.B. Students will doubtless suggest many other equally good possible headlines. What is important is that they should be graphic and eye-catching as this is the function of headlines.

Exercises 2–5   **Classroom treatment** It is recommended that each student writes the answers to these exercises and that they are then checked with the class as a whole. In this way each student performs every part of each task.

Answers

Exercise 2   1 False; 2 False; 3 True; 4 False; 5 False

Exercise 3   1 rejecting; disruptive; indifferent; oblivious; antagonistic
2 worried; despairing; completely baffled; extremely sad

Exercise 4   1 tramp; 2 2½; 3 back; 4 £60; 5 Cockney

Exercise 5   1: reading for gist; 2: reading for detail; 3: reading for inference; 4: scanning for specific information

Exercise 6   **Classroom treatment** You could use the following as discussion prompts if they are needed:
   – What would you have done in the same circumstances?
   – Would it have done John any good to stay at home?
   – Can he possibly be helped at all in care?
   – Do you think John will ever forgive his parents for putting him in care?

Grammar   This grammar pattern is frequently tested in Section A of the Use of English Paper. It is also of great use to students in composition writing and discussion work. At this level students must be able to operate beyond simple sentences and be able to use and understand complex sentences. Both versions of this pattern are equally correct
e.g. My parents don't like me/Peter coming in late.
   My parents don't like my/Peter's coming in late.
The second version, however, is more formal than the first. This should be pointed out to students.

Classroom treatment

Exercise 1   This exercise could just be done orally round the class.

Exercise 2   This exercise could be done initially in writing to provide written consolidation and then a number of the sentences could be read out.

Exercise 3   After each student has made his/her two lists, he/she could discuss, explain and justify his/her opinions with a partner in pairs. It might then be interesting to see if there is any consensus round the class as to the things they approve or disapprove of other people doing.

Coursebook pp 14–15

The discursive composition Discursive compositions are just one of the three kinds of compositions students may be asked to write in the Composition Paper. The other two are dealt with in Units 7 and 12. Discursive compositions are those which involve discussion of the arguments surrounding a particular issue. The composition title may be phrased so as to require students to give their own opinions or else to outline the general arguments concerning a particular issue. This kind of composition requires logical progression from one point to the next, and thus it becomes very important for students to write a plan to ensure this progression. It also frequently requires the use of introductory phrases such as those on page 15, and joining words such as those on pages 16 and 17.

The questions of style, register and paragraphing are not developed in this Unit, though they are as relevant to this kind of composition writing as to any other. They are dealt with in Units 7 and 12, at which point students could be encouraged to see the relevance of these questions to all kinds of composition writing.

We consider good planning to be one of the keys to good composition writing, and it is for this reason that several exercises concentrate just on planning.

Exercise 1 **Classroom treatment** You may want to ask students to read this exercise for home study. However, as it is most important to guarantee that all students do in fact read these pages and also have the opportunity to voice any query they may have, we recommend that it is read in class. Try particularly to get students to remember the four steps in composition writing — *read the title, plan, write, check.* To practise the use of the words and expressions on page 15 you could ask students to give you their opinion on various issues e.g. military service for women, smoking in public, cable TV, the Eurovision Song Contest.

Exercise 2 As indicated in the Coursebook. N.B. Step 2 will probably provoke quite a lot of discussion between partners. This is good as it forces students to reconsider their arguments.

Possible answers

1 The plan for this composition will obviously vary with each student's opinions. However, its basic pattern will probably be

Para. 1 – introduction
Para. 2 – reasons why parents should look after their children
Para. 3 – situations in which it may not be parents' duty to look after their children
Para. 4 – conclusion

N.B. The order of paragraphs 2 and 3 can be reversed.

3 The contents of this plan will vary too according to students' opinions, but it will again probably fall into two parts in addition to the introduction and the conclusion; one part in which the students give their opinions on guidance and correction, and the other part in which they give their opinion on punishment.

Coursebook pp 16–17

Listening 'Substitute Parents' This section is intended both for listening comprehension work and as a lead-in to discussion.

Style of text: serious, factual, knowledgeable

Register: neutral

Focus vocabulary

to go to the dogs: to deteriorate badly (used with people, organisations, etc.)
single-parent families: families in which there is only one parent, for whatever reason
dual-career families: families in which both parents hold a full-time job
a toddler: a child who has just learnt to walk

Exercise 1 **Classroom treatment** Use this discussion to lead into the listening comprehension as follows, for example:

– Should John's teachers have helped him more?
– Is it a teacher's job to help students sort their problems out or should they just teach their subjects?
– Can a social worker ever make a satisfactory substitute for a parent?
– How on earth can you explain what happened to John?

Exercise 2 **Classroom treatment** For this gist listening exercise just play the tape straight through *without* pausing.

Exercise 3 **Classroom treatment** Students should be advised just to write notes as answers, i.e. one or two words only and *not* complete sentences. The answers to these questions come in fairly rapid succession. It is recommended therefore that this detailed listening should be done as follows:

1 Play the tape straight through *without* pausing while students begin to take notes.
2 Students check answers in pairs.
3 Play the tape through again pausing after each answer is given on the tape so students can check or alter their answers.
4 Check the answers with the class as a whole.

Tapescript

TUTOR: Unit 2. Generations. Look at page 16, Exercise 2. You're going to hear a radio interview with a sociologist. Listen to find out his general views about the family today and about substitute parents. Ready?

INTER-VIEWER: We seem to be hearing more and more nowadays about 'the breakup of the family', that 'parents aren't as good as they used to be' or that 'the lack of good old-fashioned family life is one of the main causes of the rise in juvenile crime'. To look at the family and the role of parents in this day and age, we've invited to the studio Dr Neil, a well-known sociologist. Dr Neil, are parents 'worse' than they used to be? *Is* the family breaking up?

DR NEIL: Well, let's remember first of all that people have been saying for years that 'the family and family life's going to the dogs'. But in spite of that, I think family life *is* different now, and noticeably different.

INTER.: In what way?

DR NEIL: In a number of ways. You see, in addition to a substantial increase in divorce in many countries, um fewer people are getting re-married.

INTER.: So you're saying that there are now more one-parent or single-parent families.

DR NEIL: Oh, yes, most definitely. Far more than there ever used to be. But mm not only are there more one-parent families, but families in general seem to be smaller. And the reason(s) for that are numerous.

INTER.: Nevertheless, there must also be other differences between family life now and that of, say, thirty or forty years ago. What about the families in which both parents go out to work?

DR NEIL: Yes. 'Dual career' families, as we call them, are much more common. And what's more, parents who both want to continue

25

with their careers often do so when their children are still very young indeed.

INTER.: Yes, we receive a lot of letters from people who disapprove of mothers going on with full-time careers while their children are still toddlers. But besides these differences, I know that you have recently highlighted in some of your research yet another way in which the family unit is different now.

DR NEIL: Yes, the 'substitute parent'. More and more parents, certainly er well in the United States and in England and other European countries, are paying more people to look after their children. They're paying for substitutes, if you like.

INTER.: You mean, like baby-sitters, play groups and so on.

DR NEIL: Yes, but there are other substitutes as well of course. Teachers, youth club leaders, . . .

INTER.: And television, in its own way.

DR NEIL: Most definitely.

INTER.: Let's go back to teachers for the moment. Um primary school teachers have always really had er er a substitute parent role, haven't they? Whereas the teachers of older children teach reading, writing and academic subjects, the primary school teacher has always reinforced what the parents are doing – helping children to acquire good habits and so on. As well as perhaps to start them reading and writing.

DR NEIL: Yes, and sometimes the situation has created confusion.

INTER.: Oh, you mean, because of different 'messages' that children might be getting from parents and teachers.

DR NEIL: Yes.

INTER.: There are people now of course who think that, because of more parents going out to work, teachers of older children should take on – or at least be aware of the fact that they are parent substitutes.

DR NEIL: Yes, there are people who think that. But it's very difficult because of the amount of time teachers have in which to teach what they have to teach.

INTER.: Can we go back for a moment to smaller families, which we mentioned earlier? Are there perhaps any noticeable effects of smaller families?

DR NEIL: Yes, the main thing, I think, is that there's less mixing of ages. It's said, for example, that girls learn to be parents by being involved with younger children . . .

INTER.: And fewer children are mixing with younger children.

DR NEIL: Yes.

INTER.: But that's not of primary importance, I would have thought. It seems to me that what a child really needs is a loving environment – and you can't get that when the TV is the substitute parent, for instance.

DR NEIL: Yes, television worries me. A child needs basic trust and love and a commitment from a human being. All the other substitutes – baby-sitters, play group and primary school teachers, youth club leaders and so on – fine. In their own way, and to varying degrees, they can all offer a child love and understanding. But not not the square screen!

INTER.: In other words, you don't mind other *people* looking after your children –

DR NEIL: No.

INTER.: – but you object to television taking over your role.

DR NEIL: Yes. What I'm objecting to is the economic situation which forces' many parents to go out to work and doesn't allow them to spend as much time with their children as I think parents ought to.

INTER.: Well, perhaps before we pursue this further, we should open our phone-lines for listeners to ring in . . .

TUTOR: Now rewind the tape and look at Exercise 3.
Listen again and make notes.

TUTOR: And that's the end of Unit 2.

Exercise 2   Answers

The sociologist thinks that in general families today are different from those of the past in that they are smaller and there are more and more substitute parents. Dr Neil thinks substitute parents are fine as long as they provide children with love and understanding, something which TV, one kind of substitute parent, can't.

Exercise 3   1   It has been going to the dogs.
2a   There is a substantial increase in divorce.
 b   Remarriage is less common.
 c   Single-parent families are increasing in number.
 d   There are many more dual-career families than previously.
3   They disapprove of them, particularly of mothers going out to work while their children are still toddlers.
4   Baby-sitters, playgroups, teachers, youth club leaders, TV.
5   Because girls learn to be parents by being involved with younger children.

Exercise 4   **Classroom treatment** It may be that the listening comprehension provokes
Discussion   spontaneous discussion of the issues it contains or of John's case, at which rate this discussion may not need to be done. The teacher should try to lead into the discussion naturally after the listening comprehension i.e. without referring students to Exercise 4. The following could be used as discussion prompts if they are needed:
– Do you know any problem children?
– Why do you think they become as they are?
– Are there really problem children or are they just children with 'growing up problems'?
– What would you have done if you had been John's parents at each stage in his sad story?

Vocabulary   These joining words help students to produce complex sentences. As such they are useful for the Composition and Interview Papers. They are also items which can be tested in Section A of the Reading Comprehension Paper and the Use of English Paper. Students must learn not only the meaning of these words but also their register and the grammatical construction which each takes.

Exercises 1 and 2   **Classroom treatment** Each student should write the answers in his notebook and then the correct answers could be written up on the blackboard.

Exercise 3   **Classroom treatment** This exercise should also be done individually first of all, so that all students have to think about the language and concepts involved. A class check of answers can then follow.

Exercises 1 and 3   **Answers**

1 Whereas he promised he would behave, in fact he quickly went back to his old ways. (F)
2 On the one hand he promised he would behave but on the other in fact he quickly . . . (F)
3 Much though he promised he would behave, in fact he quickly . . . (F)
4 He promised he would behave. However, in fact he quickly . . . (F)
5 Despite promising/having promised that he would behave, in fact he quickly . . . (F)
6 He promised he would behave. Nevertheless, in fact he quickly . . . (F)
7 In spite of that fact that he promised he would behave, in fact he quickly . . . (F)

8 Although he promised he would behave, in fact he quickly . . . (N)

9 While he promised he would behave, in fact he quickly . . . (N)

10 He promised he would behave, yet in fact he quickly . . . (N)

Other 'contrast' words: *but, though*

Exercise 2 1 Not only had John met some skinheads but he had also been sniffing glue. (N/F)

2 In addition to meeting/having met some skinheads, John had also been . . . (N)

3 John had met some skinheads. Moreover, he had been . . . (F)

4 Besides meeting/having met some skinheads John had also been . . . (N)

5 John had met some skinheads. What's more, he had been . . . (N)

Other 'addition' words: *furthermore, and*

Test Composition It is recommended that this test be done in class. If however class time is short, it could be done at home. It is important that students learn to do compositions in the required time. The hour allowed for the composition breaks down approximately as follows: 5 mins. – reading instructions and composition titles + thinking time. 10 mins. – planning, 35 mins. – writing, 10 mins. – checking. It is worth pointing out to students this breakdown of the hour even at this early stage in the course so that they get used to working within these time constraints.

Suggested marking scheme Give an impression mark on a 0–5 scale for each of the following factors, where 0 = very poor, and 5 = excellent:

Grammatical accuracy:	0	1	2	3	4	5
Range and accuracy of vocabulary:	0	1	2	3	4	5
Appropriacy of style:	0	1	2	3	4	5
Relevance of content to the composition title:	0	1	2	3	4	5
Fluency and naturalness of language:	0	1	2	3	4	5
Required length:	0	1	2	3	4	5
Quality of argument:	0	1	2	3	4	5
Spelling:	0	1	2	3	4	5

Total possible score for whole test: 40

N.B. The Cambridge Examinations Syndicate works on a pass mark of approximately 40%, i.e. 8/20.

UNIT 3 Mysteries and Theories

Aims of the Unit 1 To introduce students to summarising what they have read (or heard). This is in preparation for the summary in Section B of the Use of English Paper (and for the discussion part of the Interview Paper).
2 To introduce students to the blank-filling testing technique that appears as Exercise 1 in Section A of the Use of English Paper.
3 Grammar: to review some uses of the definite article *the*.
4 To expand students' knowledge of vocabulary connected to the topic of *Mysteries and Theories*.

Coursebook pp 18–19

Exercise 1 This exercise is intended to whet the students' appetite for the following text and the rest of the Unit.

Classroom treatment Encourage students to provide as much information as they can on any of these mysteries and try to prove, disprove or explain what seem like conflicting theories or evidence. Prompt if necessary with questions such as: What is the /Bermuda Triangle/? What is strange about it? What have you heard about it? How do you account for it?, etc.

Exercise 2 The purpose of this passage, taken from a book of mysteries of the world, is to establish the background of events before students go on to discuss the rival theories and explanations. As it is, therefore, only a lead-in to what follows, it should not take up too much class time.

Style of text: journalese, colourful

Register: neutral

Focus vocabulary
remote: quiet and lonely; far from the city
to flatten: to make or become flat
to incinerate: to destroy something by burning
foliage: (uncountable n.) leaves on trees
to rip: to tear quickly and violently
a blast: an explosion or a very powerful rush of air caused by one
to uproot: to pull or tear up by the roots
a flash: a sudden quick bright light

Classroom treatment
1 Ask students what they know about the Siberian Mystery.
2 Students read the passage quickly just to get the gist of what happened.
3 Students report back.
4 Students read the true/false statements.
5 Students read the passage again looking for answers.

6 Students report back with their answers and argue their case by making close reference to the passage if there is any disagreement about the answers.

Answers

1 False; 2 True; 3 False; 4 False; 5 True

Exercise 3
Jigsaw reading

One purpose of this exercise is to get students to make notes in groups on two of the theories, and then, working from their notes only, to explain those theories to students from another group. It is important for the teacher to check that students' notes are well-made i.e. neither too full nor too scant. This is an important step in summary work. A second purpose is to encourage students to work together to decipher a text and thus use their own brain power rather than the teacher's. A third purpose is to prepare for the Interview Paper. (See N.B.)

N.B. Jigsaw reading is one of the possible forms of the Structured Comunication Exercises that make up the third part of the Interview Paper. Jigsaw reading involves a number of students each reading a different part of the same text (e.g. a story), and then through a process of oral question and answer and relating their parts of the text to one another, gradually pooling their knowledge of the text, so that in the end they all know and understand the whole of it.

Style of text: objective, report-like

Register: formal, scientific

Focus vocabulary

to level: to make or become flat and even
radial: arranged like a wheel; with bars, lines, etc. coming from one centre
to scorch: to burn a surface so as to change its colour
to billow: to swell out, as a sail
a crater: a hole in the ground formed by an explosion
to detect: to notice

Classroom treatment

1 Make sure students understand what is required of them. Tell them to ask one another in *English* or work out from the context the meaning of new vocabulary and only to ask the teacher as a last resort.

Exercise 3 1

2 Divide the students into groups of three or four as indicated.
3 Students read and take notes.

Exercise 3 2

4 Students re-form into new groups to tell one another about the theories they have just read.

Exercise 3 3

5 Still in the same groups students discuss Exercise **3** 3.

N.B. During steps 3 and 4 the teacher should check that students are only focusing on the main parts of the theories.

Coursebook p 20

Summary writing
Exercise 1

This may be the first time some students have ever done summary writing. Both these and other students may therefore appreciate some discussion on the purpose of summary writing, which is to say succinctly what has previously or elsewhere been said or written at greater length: a report of a meeting, a description of the story line of a film, a TV news résumé of a politician's speech, telling your mother/husband about your day at work or college are all examples of summarising that students will be familiar with in their everyday lives. It is important that students don't see summary writing purely as an academic exercise, but as something that we constantly do almost every day, as this helps them to appreciate the relevance of gist and main points. We summarise because we don't have the time, space, means or interest in repeating the whole episode or event over again.

Classroom treatment

1 Discuss the purpose of summary writing as indicated above.
2 You might refer students immediately to the first two theories on page 19 and ask them as a class to tell you what the main points of the two theories are. Write the points on the blackboard.
3 Compare the points on the blackboard with those outlined on page 20.
4 Ask students to read the summary and note down differences between it and the main points.
5 Students report back.
6 Ask students to substitute other suitable connectors for those used in the summary.
7 Ask students to make other oral summaries of the same main points using different joining words and possibly different sentence constructions.

Exercise 2   **Classroom treatment** Read this information over with the students.

Exercise 3   As this may be the first summary students have done, it is advisable for them to do it in class so that the teacher can give them immediate feedback as to whether they are on the right lines or not.
N.B. There will of course be different final versions of the summary.

Classroom treatment Make sure students follow the procedure outlined in Exercise 2. The teacher could interrupt this procedure after steps 2, 3 and 6 for checking purposes or get students to check their work in pairs after the same steps.

Suggested answers Main points for the summary:
3rd theory: – put forward in 1946 by Alexander Kazantsev
            – says earth hit by nuclear explosion on board spaceship
            – this theory would account for various phenomena noted after explosion
4th theory: – comet hit earth and caused nuclear explosion
            – comet not observed because arrived early morning in path of Sun's rays
N.B. These main points are written in note form as a student's should be.

Coursebook p 21

Grammar   Even for students at this level of English, the use of the Definite Article *the* causes
Exercise 1   considerable problems. It may be necessary to revise more basic concepts of the use of *the* with students i.e. that *the* defines particular things, but is not used when we want to talk about things in general. This section, however, is designed to summarise the use or absence of *the* when talking about places, names and periods of time. Students' attention should be drawn to the names of planets, places, names of people, magazines, etc. which occurred in the texts on pages 18–19.

Classroom treatment Read the information through with the students or ask them to study it silently for five minutes or so, *or* set it as a home study section (together with Exercise 2). If done in class you might ask questions like the following to establish some of the uses of *the*, for example:
What other planets do you know?
Which continents/countries/cities have you visited? When?

What places have been in the news recently? Why?
Which summer/winter do you remember best? Why?, etc.

Exercise 2   **Classroom treatment** It's best if each student writes the answers to the whole exercise, then checks his answers with a partner and then the whole class checks with the teacher. This procedure guarantees that everyone takes part in every stage of the activity.

Answers

We came screaming in towards *the* solar system from *the* outer reaches of *the* Milky Way. We had been away a long time, a very long time, but we calculated that down on Earth it was Easter Sunday, 2095.
The Sun, our very own Sun, was in view: then on through *the* system past Neptune, Jupiter, Mars and *the* other planets until (*the*) Earth and *the* Moon came clearly into view on our screens. There was silence in *the* ship, each crew member with his or her own thoughts. And as we drew nearer and prepared to orbit Mother Earth, we could make out *the* Atlantic, *the* Arctic and *the* continents of Europe and Asia. Nearer still, and we could clearly distinguish other familiar features — *the* Himalayas, *the* Mediterranean Sea and *the* Nile, *the* British Isles, Italy and *the* Iberian Peninsula. And I imagined *the* people in Scandinavia, Africa and *the* USSR watching for our return. Yet as we drew nearer still, features in detail were not so familiar, and I had a dread of what we might find.

Listening   This task has a similar purpose to the *Siberian Mystery* tasks in that it aims to get students to select information, summarise and report. The difference here, clearly, is that the information is provided in the spoken and not in the written mode.

Style of text: factual

Register: neutral

Focus vocabulary

a lifeboat: one of the small boats carried by a ship for escape in case of wreck, fire, etc.
a hold: the part of a ship (below deck) where goods are stored
insanity: madness
piracy: robbery by pirates i.e. people who sail the seas stopping and robbing ships
fungus: simple fast-spreading plants with a powderlike appearance, considered as a disease
timbers: wooden beams, esp. curved pieces forming part of a ship's framework
overboard: over the side of a ship or boat into the water
plausible: seeming to be true or reasonable

Classroom treatment As indicated in the Coursebook, followed by a class discussion of what the students think could have happened in the mystery of the Mary Celeste.

📼 Tapescript

TUTOR: Unit 3. Mysteries and Theories. Look at page 21. Listening. You're going to hear a radio interview with an author. Listen and make notes on the facts of what happened and on the different theories. Ready?

INTER-VIEWER: That record was for Susan in Oxford. And now for our 'Meet The Authors' spot this week, and I'm pleased to have with me the author of a new book on mysteries of the world, Mark Taylor. Good evening, Mark.

MARK: Good evening.

INTER.:   Now, lots of people nowadays seem to be interested in the mysterious, the weird and wonderful, and so on . . .

MARK: Yes, they are, and that's obviously one reason why I wrote the book.

INTER.:   Well, I've read the book and it really is quite fascinating. It's full of accounts of strange happenings, but you've rethought many of the theories that have been put forward to date, haven't you.

MARK: Yes, I have. And I suppose I have been overcritical of some of the explanations that have been suggested to account for certain happenings and events in the past. But there is one that's so extraordinary that all I have been able to do is restate what others have said before.

INTER.:   And which is that? The Curse of the Pharaohs?

MARK: No, I'm talking about the mystery of the 'Mary Celeste'.

INTER.:   Ah. Well, could you tell us some of the theories about what might have happened on that ship?

MARK: Yes, of course. But in view of the time at my disposal I'll have to oversimplify things a little. Briefly the facts are these: In October, 1872, the 'Mary Celeste', she was a cargo sailing ship, set sail from New York for Genoa under Captain Briggs. On board were his wife and 2-year-old daughter, and 8 crew. A month later, the ship was found sailing around erratically in the Azores by a Captain Moorhouse who was sailing his ship to Gibraltar. The 'Mary Celeste' was abandoned, deserted. The one lifeboat was missing, as were the navigation instruments and the ship's papers, and there was some water in the hold, but all the cargo was intact. Everything seemed to have been left behind as if everyone had left in a great hurry.

INTER.:   Strange, isn't it?

MARK: Yes, you see the real mystery is: why was the ship completely abandoned, and if the crew escaped in the lifeboat, why didn't they take provisions with them?

INTER.:   Hmm.

MARK: Well, there are almost dozens of theories, but they all kind of fall under three headings: firstly, illness or insanity; secondly, violence or piracy, which was not unknown then; and thirdly, crisis at sea.

INTER.:   Well, what about illness or insanity as a possible explanation?

MARK: Well, it's been suggested that everyone on board was poisoned somehow, either by fungus in the bread, or a poisonous gas either from fungus in the ship's timbers or even from the sea. At any rate, the suggestion is that they were all driven mad and jumped overboard or tried to escape in the lifeboat. Like all the explanations, it's possible, I suppose.

INTER.:   But you also mentioned insanity.

MARK: Yes, it has been suggested that the captain, who was fervently religious, by the way, basically went mad and murdered everyone and then threw himself into the sea. Well, I don't think that's very plausible but there's nothing to disprove it.

INTER.:   How about the violence or piracy theories?

MARK: One of the 'violence' theories suggests that the crew drank some of the alcohol which the ship was carrying, then murdered the captain and his family, then, when they realised what they'd done, they dropped the bodies overboard and abandoned the ship in the lifeboat. It's a theory.

INTER.:   You sound doubtful about all the theories you've given us to date. What about the 'crisis at sea' solution?

MARK: Well, this makes much better sense, in my view, but the whole problem with the mystery is you can't prove or disprove anything completely. I personally think there was a crisis of some kind. One suggestion is that one of the sailors went down into the hold and found water in it. Thinking that the ship was sinking, or was going to sink, he shouted the alarm and everyone rushed for the lifeboat and abandoned ship as quickly as possible. There are a number of objections to that theory as there are with all the others.

INTER.:   It's a fascinating mystery, Mark, but I'm afraid that's all we've time for. So I'd just like to thank you for coming to the studio today and to recommend . . .

TUTOR: If you wish to listen to the interview again, rewind the tape.

TUTOR: And that's the end of Unit 3.

Possible answers Main points only:

What happened: Ship set sail for Genoa from New York in 1872. On board were captain, wife, daughter and 8 crew. Ship found abandoned month later in Azores. Lifeboat, navigation instruments and ship's papers missing; water in hold; cargo intact.

1st theory: – illness; all poisoned by fungus in bread or ship's timbers or sea. As a result, went mad and jumped overboard or tried to escape in lifeboat.

2nd theory: – insanity; captain (fervently religious) went mad, murdered everyone and threw self in sea. Theory not very plausible.

3rd theory: – violence; crew drank alcohol, then murdered captain and family, then when realised what had done, dropped bodies overboard and abandoned ship in lifeboat.

4th theory: – crisis at sea; member of crew saw water in hold, thought ship was sinking, so shouted alarm and everyone abandoned ship in the lifeboat.

Coursebook p 22

Reading and filling in blanks

Exercise 1

This page introduces students to the technique of blank-filling, which is the technique employed in Section A of the Use of English Paper, as well as to a way of approaching such tests. Students are often worried and perplexed by this technique; however, familiarity with it will help them greatly to be able to cope with it. It might even be an idea to introduce them to this technique by giving them a short passage with blanks in their own language, asking them to complete the blanks and then to verbalise the mental processes they employed to arrive at the answers. The same processes are of course valid when working in English.

To do such tests successfully it is vital that students:

1 *read the whole passage through first* to get its general meaning.
2 read the words and/or sentences both *before* and *after* each blank when attempting to fill them in.
3 look for both grammatical and semantic clues to the answers.
4 be prepared to leave a blank unanswered, then return to it once the succeeding blank(s) is/are completed. It may well be that the following sentence(s) will help them to understand the previous one.

Classroom treatment

1 Start by building students' confidence in their ability to handle tests like this by explaining to them that the more they do this kind of test the easier they will find them and also perhaps by getting them to do a blank-filling exercise in their own language as indicated above.
2 Read through steps 1, 2 and 3 with the students.

Exercise 2 **Classroom treatment**

1 Ask the students to read the passage through for gist.
2 Check students' gist understanding.
3 Work through some of the questions about the first few blanks with the students.
4 Students complete the exercise on their own or in pairs.
5 Check students' answers.

Answers

1 for/of; 2 so; 3 up; 4 which/that; 5 over/through/across; 6 out; 7 by; 8 then/always/ invariably; 9 who/that; 10 in/through; 11 the/some/fresh; 12 in; 13 most; 14 of; 15 forward; 16 the; 17 protect/secure; 18 could/might/may; 19 both; 20 Such/This/ That/The

Homework exercise Summary

Classroom preparation

1 Students read passage and make notes.
2 Check notes and put a series of model main points on the blackboard as suggested by students.
3 Students and teacher discuss possible ordering and linking of points and use of joining words.
4 Students are asked to write the summary for homework.

Suggested answers Main points only:

1st theory: – says tombs – perfect breeding ground for bacteria to develop new and unknown strains across the centuries and still be potent today.

2nd theory: – poison contained in wall paintings attacked visitors by penetrating their skin.

3rd theory: – atomic radiation produced by covering floor in tombs with radio-active rock.

Coursebook p 23

Test Use of English

We recommend you get students to do the test in class under exam-like conditions and in the recommended time.

Exercise 1

Answers

1 any; 2 in; 3 held; 4 for; 5 then; 6 which/that; 7 In; 8 the; 9 It; 10 in/during; 11 on/ by/near; 12 from; 13 Because; 14 was; 15 but; 16 which; 17 whose; 18 causing; 19 the/this/that; 20 told/recounted

Exercise 2

Suggested answers Main points only:

How tested suspicions –	tried to see if Flambeau would show himself by
	1 changing salt for sugar in Flambeau's coffee;
	2 altering Flambeau's bill to three times too much.
Subsequent course of action -	1 got cross returned to Westminster;
	2 attracted police's attention by splashing a wall, spilling apples and breaking a window.

Suggested marking scheme

Exercise 1: Allot one mark for each correct item to give a possible maximum of 20.

Exercise 2: Mark out of 30, allotting marks on a 0–5 scale for:

correct information:	0	1	2	3	4	5
well-joined sentences:	0	1	2	3	4	5
correct grammar:	0	1	2	3	4	5
appropriate style:	0	1	2	3	4	5
accurate vocabulary:	0	1	2	3	4	5
accurate spelling:	0	1	2	3	4	5

Total possible score for whole test: 50 marks.

UNIT 4 Crime and Punishment

PAPER 4: **LISTENING COMPREHENSION**

Aims of the Unit
1 To introduce students to a range of 'non-standard' English accents.
2 To develop the skill of listening for detail.
3 To familiarise students with material presented in visual forms (e.g. a chart, a graph).
4 To show students how to use listening comprehension task sheets to predict the content of recorded material.
5 Grammar: to review some adjective and adverb constructions.
6 To expand students' knowledge of vocabulary connected to the topic of *Crime and Punishment*.

Coursebook pp 24–25

Exercise 1 **Classroom treatment** As indicated in the Coursebook. The following could be used as discussion prompts if they are needed:

– Has there been a rise in mugging, bank robberies, etc.?
– Do you think the present economic situation has contributed to the crime situation?
– Are there really more crimes or are statistics more accurate?

Exercise 2 The Listening Comprehension Paper may require students to listen to non-standard
1a) 1b) English accents and this is why this Unit contains a focus on accents. The more students are exposed to non-standard accents, the more easily they will be able to cope with them. Like much else, dealing with accents is a question of familiarity. In this Unit students are asked to recognise accents not because this is a task they will have to perform in the exam (they won't), but because this task acts as a way of helping students to deal with accents more confidently.

Classroom treatment As indicated in the Coursebook. It may also be useful to ask students to try to say what they perceive the difference between the various accents to be; again just so as to increase their confidence. Pause after each accent to do this.

1b) **Tapescript**

TUTOR:	Now look at page 24, Exercise 1b. You're going to hear extracts from a newspaper article read by people with different 'non-standard' English accents. As you listen, write in the number of the speaker against the accent. Ready? One.
SCOTTISH:	During the past few years, town and city planners in Britain have been drawing up plans for the city environment of the future. Their main concern is to eliminate weak spots, hiding places and temptation in order to reduce the amount of vandalism, mugging and burglary.

TUTOR:	Two.
AUSTRALIAN:	Criminals need hiding places, such as tall hedges, fences, doorways, and so on, so the city environment of the future will have wide open spaces. And paths and other pedestrian areas will be lit at night with streetlights that should be vandal-proof.
TUTOR:	Three.
WELSH:	Security will be one of the prime considerations in the design of buildings. Visitors to blocks of flats or private houses will be checked either by caretakers or by remote control television monitors.
TUTOR:	Four.
AMERICAN:	All of these proposed measures, and there are many more, will be put together under three new British Standards – one for dwellings, another for commercial and industrial premises, and a third for public places.
TUTOR:	Five.
CARIBBEAN:	Work began back in 1982 with the first meeting of a new British Standards Institute committee. Represented were members of the police, the security and insurance industries, local authorities, surveyors, architects, fire officers, and many more.
TUTOR:	Six.
SOUTH AFRICAN:	The aim of this new BSI committee is to produce what is in effect a comprehensive security blueprint. In one document, it hopes to reproduce all the available information on vandal-proof street furniture, locks, and security doors and windows.
TUTOR:	Seven.
IRISH:	In the future, every citizen will not be regarded as innocent and law-abiding. Instead, in order to lead a trouble-free daily life, he will have to be prepared to prove his innocence. In an attempt to deter terrorist bombers, the citizens . . .
TUTOR:	Now rewind the tape, listen again and check your answers with a partner and the class.

Answers

South African 6; American 4; Scottish 1; Irish 7; Welsh 3; Caribbean 5; Australian 2

2a) 2b) When we listen to spoken language in everyday life we normally have some idea of what we are going to listen to, we know what the subject matter is going to be and sometimes, depending on who is speaking and what about, we can even go so far as to predict what they are going to say with some accuracy. This ability to predict helps us to understand what is being said. In real life we base our ability to predict on clues such as facial expression, where the text or conversation takes place, who it is spoken by and what we know about the people speaking and the particular topic. When listening to a tape these clues are of course not available in the same form, but much can nevertheless be predicted by looking at questions, task sheets, etc. If students come to realise how much support they can get from these, it will not only help them immediately with their listening but will also build up their confidence.

2b) **Tapescript**

TUTOR:	Now look at page 24, Exercise 2b. You're going to hear someone talking about the rise in crime. As you listen, fill in the missing information in the four boxes. Don't worry if you miss something the first time.
WOMAN:	Sad though it is, we have to admit that crime is on the increase, especially in large cities like London. Not only have muggings, burglaries and car thefts become more and more common, but *all* crimes apparently. These are the frightening figures for *all crimes* committed in London: there were 354,445 recorded crimes in London back in 1972. By 1982, only ten years later, that figure

had more than doubled to a staggering 688,179. 688,179! But the most frightening of all is the almost unbelievable, and very worrying rise in *armed robbery* over the same period, from 380 recorded cases in 1972 to not far off 2,000 in 1982. To be precise, there were 1,772 recorded cases of armed robbery in London in that year. That's 400 per cent more than were committed ten years before!

TUTOR: Now rewind the tape, listen again and check your answers with a partner and the class.

Suggested answers

Predictions: 1 that someone will be talking about a ten-year period of crime in a capital city
2 in box 1 a starting figure, probably about 300–400
in box 3 a top figure; probably about 650,000
3 boxes 2 and 4 probably tell us what kind of crime each graph refers to; otherwise the graphs wouldn't make sense by themselves

Actual answers: Box 1 380; Box 3 688,179; Box 2 Armed robbery; Box 4 All crimes

Exercise 3
Listening

Style of text: straightforward, opinion

Register: neutral

🔊 Tapescript

TUTOR: Look at page 25, Exercise 2.
You're going to hear two people being interviewed in the street as part of an opinon poll to discover the attitudes of the general public to certain social problems.
As you listen, fill in the chart as if you were the interviewer. Mark 'M' for the man's opinions, and 'W' for the woman's. Ready?

INTER-
VIEWER: Now the next question.

MAN: Yes.

INTER.: I'm going to read out a list of crimes and for each one I'd like you to tell me which of the sentences on the card you feel should represent the *maximum* sentence imposed by the courts.

MAN: Hmm . . . hmm . . .

INTER.: Bigamy.

MAN: Oh . . . . . . don't know, really.

INTER.: Blackmail?

MAN: Well, that's becoming a lot more common. Certainly a sentence of some kind . . . imprisonment . . . Oh, seven or eight years.

INTER.: Mm. Possession of drugs?

MAN: About the same. Perhaps a little longer. Say ten years. I must say I'm absolutely disgusted at the way people like that spread . . . um . . .

INTER.: Yes. Hijacking?

MAN: Hijacking? Oh, about 15 years in prison. Definitely.

INTER.: Kidnapping?

MAN: The same. 15 years.

INTER.: Murder.

MAN: You couldn't have a list of crimes without murder, could you? Life. Life imprisonment. And by that, I mean for the rest of the murderer's life. Not let out for good behaviour after ten years.

INTER.: Armed robbery?

MAN: Ten years.

INTER.: Theft, including shoplifting.

MAN: Oh, including shoplifting. That's difficult. I would have said 'no sentence' for shoplifting: at least, not a prison sentence. I don't know. Perhaps a year or so.

INTER.: Rape and other sexual offences.

MAN: Life. No doubt about it. Life in prison. I think a lot of people are deeply disturbed at the way these particular crimes have increased in recent years.

INTER.: And lastly, mugging.

MAN: Well, I'd put that on a level with armed robbery and say at least ten years. No, more: at least 12 years.

INTER.: Thank you. Now there's just one more question . . .

TUTOR: Now listen to the second person being interviewed.

INTER.: . . . which of the sentences on the card you feel should represent the *maximum* sentence imposed by the courts. The first is bigamy.

WOMAN: Bigamy? Ah . . . well, I think it's an utterly despicable thing for a man to do in Britain, marry two wives. It's different in other societies, isn't it? Oh, I don't know. Five years in prison, perhaps.

INTER.: Blackmail.

WOMAN: Fifteen years, I'd say.

INTER.: And possession of drugs?

WOMAN: The same. About 15 years.

INTER.: Hijacking?

WOMAN: I find the rise in hijackings round the world absolutely appalling. And I think the only way to stop it is to impose the maximum prison sentence you can: life.

INTER.: Kidnapping.

WOMAN: It's the same story, although it's obviously a great deal worse in some countries than in others. Nevertheless, in my opinion, life imprisonment is the only answer. The sentence should at least act as a deterrent.

INTER.: And murder?

WOMAN: The death penalty.

INTER.: Armed robbery.

WOMAN: About fifteen or twenty years in prison, I think. After all, it's the one crime which has almost certainly risen – sorry, increased more than any other in the past few years. Perhaps longer terms of imprisonment, or at least the threat of longer sentences, might help reduce the number of armed robberies.

INTER.: Theft, including shoplifting.

WOMAN: I would say something like six, seven, eight years, depending on the crime, the amount stolen and so on. Even shoplifters should receive much longer sentences than they do. I'm absolutely amazed at the way shoplifters – thieves – are often let off scot-free. At least that's what I think.

INTER.: Rape and sexual assault.

WOMAN: Again the frequency of these kind of crimes is frightening. But I really don't know what the answer is, and I honestly don't know what sentence a rapist should be given in court. I wish I did, but I just don't know.

INTER.: And finally, mugging.

WOMAN: Mugging. There was a case in the papers the other day where an old lady in her 80s was mugged by two youths and badly beaten – just for a few pounds. They've got to give muggers life. Definitely life.

INTER.: Thank you. Now there's just one more question . . .

TUTOR: If you wish to listen to the interview again, rewind the tape.

Answers

1 The chart is probably part of an interviewer's questionnaire as it has the same format as a questionnaire, and the words in quotation marks in the chart talk about a card which will be shown to people by someone who must be an interviewer or marker researcher.

We're probably going to hear a dialogue between an interviewer and someone in the street. The interviewer will be unlikely to enter into a discussion as he wants precise answers.

The tape could help a listener to understand the meaning of particular crimes because the people interviewed might make some comment on the crimes.

	MAN	WOMAN
Bigamy	Don't know	2–5 years
Blackmail	6–10 years	11 years to life
Possession of drugs	6–10 years	11 years to life
Hijacking	11 years to life	Life sentence
Kidnapping	11 years to life	Life sentence
Murder	Life sentence	Death penalty
Armed robbery	6–10 years	11 years to life
Theft (incl. shoplifting)	Under 2 years	6–10 years
Rape and other sexual offences	Life sentence	Don't know
Mugging	11 years to life	Life sentence

Coursebook pp 26–27

Grammar These adjective and adverb constructions could be tested in Section A of the Use of English Paper.

Exercise 2 **Answers**

1 The more unemployment increases, the more crime is likely to increase too.
2 The harder you work, the more (money) you'll earn.
3 The bigger our cities become/grow, the less safe they become.
4 The more you practise, the better you'll be.
5 The longer we wait, the more disturbing the situation will become.

Vocabulary These adverb–adjective collocations will be very useful to students in their composition writing, allowing them to express more formal styles of writing when they wish to. Such collocations are also occasionally tested in Section A of the Reading Comprehension Paper. Make sure students realise that they cannot use all the adverbs in combination with all the adjectives e.g. while it is possible to say 'I was absolutely amazed' you *cannot* say 'I was absolutely disappointed'.

The discussion which is suggested as pair work after the students have listened to the tape will involve students in using a range of the expressions within the box as they try to establish exactly how the speaker sounds.

Classroom treatment As suggested in the Coursebook. Students could also be asked where they have seen or heard expressions such as 'I was greatly relieved', 'he was highly amused' and 'they were extremely annoyed', etc. as their answers to these questions will reveal to the students the formality of the expressions. It is *not* a good idea to ask students questions such as: What deeply depresses you?/What bitterly disappoints you?/When have you been utterly disgusted? etc. precisely because this language is too formal to be used in this way. Once students have done this task, they could then concentrate on the accents on the same part of the tape.

🎞 Tapescript

TUTOR: Look at page 27, Vocabulary.
You're going to hear a number of people saying things and expressing different emotions. As you listen, decide what feeling the speaker is expressing and write down a phrase to describe it e.g. 'deeply offended', 'absolutely determined', etc.

There'll be a short pause after each one to allow you to write down what you think. Ready?
One.

AMERICAN: *(absolutely amazed)* You say you've passed the exam? That's incredible! You never thought you'd pass, did you?

TUTOR: Two.

SCOT: *(deeply disappointed)* Oh no, that's really bad news. He'll be so upset. I really thought he stood a good chance. That's awful.

TUTOR: Three.

STANDARD: *(thoroughly annoyed)* Oh, for goodness' sake! Can't you get anything right?!

TUTOR: Four.

WELSH: *(utterly disgusted)* Ugh! You're not going to *eat* that, are you?! It looks *dreadful*! Ugh!

TUTOR: Five.

S. AFRICAN: *(thoroughly exhausted)* Phew! After all that exercise, I'm worn out!

TUTOR: Six.

STANDARD: *(deeply moved)* I think that must be the most moving film I've seen for a very long time. It was done so beautifully.

TUTOR: Seven.

AUSTRALIAN: *(highly amused)* That was very funny. Really – very, very funny!

TUTOR: Eight.

IRISH: *(absolutely determined)* I'm going to finish putting this table together if it's the last thing I do!

TUTOR: Nine.

CARIBBEAN: *(deeply moved)* I think that must be the most moving film I've seen for a very long time. It was done so beautifully.

TUTOR: Ten.

STANDARD: *(utterly depressed)* I just don't feel like it, that's all. I just can't be bothered . . . I don't know . . . I just don't . . . I just don't want to do anything.

TUTOR: If you wish to listen again, rewind the tape.

Answers

1 absolutely amazed; 2 deeply disappointed; 3 thoroughly annoyed; 4 utterly disgusted; 5 thoroughly exhausted; 6 deeply offended; 7 highly amused; 8 absolutely determined; 9 deeply moved; 10 utterly depressed

Coursebook pp 28–29

Homework exercises　We recommend that you ask students when doing summaries or compositions for homework to write plans for both and to hand these plans in to you together with their homework. In this way you will be able to see whether any problems they have are due to recognising and forming main topics or ideas, whether they are due to linking these, or whether to both.

Summary　**Suggested answers**

The main points should contain the following information, though the wording may well be different:

Incidence of smuggling
　　　　　– less at beginning of 19th century than in previous century. From approx. 1816 increased significantly.

Sentences – harsher than for petty crime; less harsh than for burglary or stealing bread; usually a fine; if fine not paid, were given indefinite period of imprisonment, though most were released after couple of years.

Attitudes – resentful, insubordinate, discontented

It is recommended that this test be done in class under exam-like conditions.

📼 **Tapescript**

TUTOR:	Unit 4. Listening Comprehension Test. Look at page 29, and listen.
	Part 1. Questions 1–10. You're going to hear part of a radio interview with a criminologist and will have to fill in the missing information. But before you listen, look carefully at questions 1–10.*
	Now listen and fill in the missing information. Ready?
INTER-VIEWER:	Now it is a fact, is it not, that not only is crime increasing in general but that burglaries in particular are becoming more and more common.
MAN:	That's true, certainly up to the figures we have for this year, 1983. And it's deeply disturbing. In fact, so high is the incidence of burglary in Britain that it's been calculated one house is burgled every 90 seconds. Burglaries account for nearly one quarter of all crime committed in this country.
INTER.:	That's absolutely frightening, especially when so many families have to be away from home all day at work, and school and so on, when I gather more and more burglaries are committed. During the day, I mean.
MAN:	Yes. And that may itself be a contributing factor for the annual increase in burglary. Last year, for instance, 50,000 more homes were burgled than in 1979. I don't know whether it's because more and more people are out of the house all day, or whether they are less careful about locking up thoroughly when they go out.
INTER.:	Well, the precautions that we should take against being burgled is something I'd like to discuss later, but what about the insurance situation?
MAN:	Strange as it may seem, after years of propaganda by the insurance companies, most families are still badly underinsured. During 1982 losses due to household burglary rose by 27 per cent over the previous year. So bad has the situation become, in fact, that some insurance companies are refusing to provide cover in certain high-risk areas in Britain. And that's not the end of the story, either, because the *real* number of burglaries committed in the country may be much higher than official statistics suggest. It's been calculated that some 52 per cent more burglaries are simply not reported to the police at all – or to insurance companies. Either people think that it's too trivial, or they think that the police won't be able to do anything, or they discover the burglary so long after the event – weeks or months, in some cases – that there seems little point in reporting it.
INTER.:	So you're saying that while more and more burglaries are being committed, fewer and fewer people are reporting them?
MAN:	Yes. But the trouble with statistics is that the longer you look at them, especially to do with crime, the more pessimistic you're likely to become, whereas I'd like people to become a lot more careful. The plain fact is that, if you live in Britain, you're likely to be burgled once in 40 years.
INTER.:	As you say, that doesn't sound too bad. But once in a lifetime would be plenty for most people, I'm sure.
MAN:	Yes, it can be a deeply distressing experience.
INTER.:	By the way, how much do burglars usually get away with? How much is stolen?
MAN:	Well, clearly it all depends on the circumstances. But listeners will be glad to hear that, according to a recent Survey of British Crime, 39 per cent of all burglaries are what are called 'aborted attempts'.
INTER.:	That means presumably that the burglar or burglars get nothing.

MAN: Yes. Further, 16 per cent of all burglaries result in a loss of nought to £5.

INTER.: So in over 50 per cent of all crimes the burglar gets hardly anything at all.

MAN: That's right. The highest bracket, if I can call it that, is that in which there is a loss of £5 to £99, which accounts for 22 per cent of all burglaries. Then a further 13 per cent result in losses of between £100 and £499, and the final top 13 per cent are crimes in which burglars get away with money or goods or valuables worth over £500.

INTER.: That's very interesting. But as you said earlier the experience of being burgled, whether it happens while you're at home or whether you come back to discover that you've been burgled, is a deeply disturbing one. And there are preventive measures that the average householder can take against the average burglar. Instead of talking to a policeman or crime prevention officer . . .

TUTOR: Now listen again and check your answers to questions 1–10. *(Interview repeated on tape.)*

TUTOR: Part 2. Questions 11–22. You're going to hear part of a discussion and will have to fill in the missing information. But before you listen, study the table carefully.★
Now listen and fill in the missing information. Ready?

MAN (1): . . . Well, the problem's quite obviously getting worse and worse, and it'll become more and more difficult to solve the longer it goes on. I mean, how *do* we reduce the prison population in Britain?

WOMAN: Personally, I think we've got to look at prison populations in different countries and see how they compare.

MAN (2): Can we do that?

WOMAN: It's difficult, but yes. I've brought along a table of comparisons of some European countries . . .

MAN (1): Well, let's look at that first, and then discuss some of the implications.

MAN (2): Mm, fine.

WOMAN: All right. Now if you look at the table, you'll see that the analysis was based on figures for seven countries: England and Wales, France, the Netherlands, Scotland, Sweden, Switzerland, and Northern Ireland.

MAN (1): It didn't include the Republic – Eire.

WOMAN: No. But for the countries included, the information is pretty comprehensive, as you can see from the columns. Now column A represents prison receptions per 100,000 – that's the number of people received into prisons. Column B gives the average effective sentence length in years . . .

MAN (2): Sorry, the average effective sentence length?

WOMAN: Yes. In other words, the average length of time for which people are sent to prison. Now columns C and D show the overall prison population and overall receptions respectively. And column E gives the population of the countries – population in millions, of course – and column F shows the prison population per 100,000.

MAN (1): As you say, its pretty comprehensive.

WOMAN: And quite fascinating, too. While you're looking at it, let me point out some of the um interesting aspects . . . The first thing is that under the reception rate per 100,000 (column A), England and Wales is quite low. The lowest is France with 19 – the highest is Scotland, with 129. So our reception rate – 69 – is quite low really.

MAN (2): Yes, but our average sentence length is quite high.

WOMAN: Not as high as France, where the average is 1.3 years. But you're right. With countries like the Netherlands – with 0.136 years average – we don't compare too well.

MAN (1): No, and we-we top the overall prison population league! That figure of 24,282 – 24,282! – it's quite staggering. The nearest is France with 13,000 +: that's only just over half the figure for England and Wales.

WOMAN: Well, as you'll see, we top the overall receptions too, with over 34,000. But in this case, it's the Netherlands which comes second, with 17,124. 17,124. That's surprising, isn't it?

MAN (2):   I don't know. Anyway, let's discuss that later. What surprises *me* is the population of France – 53 million.

MAN (1):   No, I never realised the population of France was that big, either.

WOMAN: I know. The number of receptions is relatively small for France too, but can we discuss population versus receptions, prison populations and so on later?

MAN (1):   By all means. Let's just look at the last column . . .

WOMAN: Yes, where it's interesting to see that Sweden is higher than England and Wales, with 50.32, and Northern Ireland tops the league with an astounding 82.33.

MAN (2):   82.33? Oh, yes. But then, that's probably only to be expected, with things as they are there.

WOMAN: Yes. Anyway, what can these figures tell us about ways that other countries have reduced their prison populations . . . ?

TUTOR: Now listen again and check your answers to questions 11–22. (*Discussion repeated on tape.*)

TUTOR: And that's the end of Unit 4 Test.

Answers

Part 1   1 90 seconds; 2 50,000; 3 27%; 4 some/about 52%; 5 once in 40 years: 6 39%; 7 16%; 8 £5 – £99; 9 £100 – £499; 10 13%.

Part 2   11 Northern Ireland; 12 average effective sentence length; 13 population of country; 14 19; 15 129; 16 1.3; 17 0.136; 18 24,282; 19 17,124; 20 53; 21 50.32; 22 82.33

Suggested marking scheme

Exercise 1: Score 1 mark each for each completely correct answer to give a possible maximum of 10 marks.

Exercise 2: Score 2 marks each for items 11, 12 and 13, and 1 mark each for items 14–22 to give a possible maximum of 15 marks.

Possible total maximum for the whole test: 25 marks.

UNIT 5 Consumer Society

Aims of the Unit
1 To familiarise students with the first part of the Interview Paper.
2 To provide students with language to deal with the photo in the Interview Paper, and with the types of questions asked about the photo by the examiner.
3 To show students how to deal with passages, as is required in the second part of the Interview Paper.
4 Grammar: to review some uses of relative pronouns and participle -*ing* form constructions.
5 To expand students' knowledge of vocabulary connected to the topic of the *Consumer Society*.

Coursebook pp 30–31

Exercise 1 This step is intended as a lead-in to the topic, grammar and vocabulary of the Unit. While it should involve and interest students it should not take up too much class time i.e. 10 minutes maximum.

Exercise 2 All the expressions listed in this exercise will, if used appropriately, allow students to sound more fluent in the Interview and also provide them with ways of dealing with those photos they might find difficult to fully understand. Students should not worry about not being able to fully understand the photos, but they should master the language which allows them to express this lack of visual comprehension. The aim of the first part of the Interview Paper is to assess students' ability to speak fluently and enter into genuine dialogue, not to see how well they can understand photos. An examiner cannot give a rather silent candidate a good mark for his oral abilities. The questions below the photos are divided into three types which correspond to the kinds of questions an examiner could ask a candidate about a photo. If students learn to recognise the kinds of questions that they might be asked, they will approach the Interview that much more confidently.

N.B. In the exam the students will not be able to see the questions.

Classroom treatment
1 Inform students that it is what they say, rather than what they see in the photo, that matters to the examiner.
2 Study the language given in Exercise **2** 1 with the students and ask them what other suitable expressions they know.
3 For Exercise **2** 2 divide the students into pairs with one student taking the role of the examiner and the other that of a candidate, and let them interview one another. (See the section on *Correction* in the General Introduction for the teacher's role during this activity.)
4 Correct any important mistakes made with the class as a whole.
5 Study the language given in Exercise **2** 3 with the class as a whole.

6 Students change pairs, with the examiner now becoming the candidate and vice versa, and do Exercise **2** 3.
7 Correction of general and important mistakes with the class as a whole.

Coursebook pp 32–33

Grammar Exercise 1 This grammar point (relative pronouns) should be merely a reminder and can therefore be looked at fairly quickly and lightly. The game is intended to practise the use of relatives and compound nouns.

1 **Classroom treatment** This exercise could be done orally round the class. It could also be turned into a guessing game; one student, for example, could choose one of the items on the list and then give a definition of it e.g. it's something that we use to tell the time. The other students would then consult the list to find the item; in this case a wristwatch. Then other students could take it in turns to give definitions of other words on the list. Point out to students that in the pronunciation of compound nouns the primary stress is on the first part.

Game: 20 questions 2 **Object of the game** To guess the identity of an item by asking no more than 20 questions.

Conduct of the game

1 Appoint a panel of three or four students and ask them to sit in front of the class.
2 Appoint a scorer who marks off on the blackboard each question as it is asked up to 20.
3 Give the rest of the students a list of e.g. 6 items (in this case they should be compound nouns e.g. a zoom lens, a remote control for the TV, a one-cup electric kettle, a pocket razor, a ticket collector, a filing clerk).
4 Taking in turn each item on the list, the panel must try to work out what each item is by asking the other students questions up to a maximum of 20. The panel can only ask Yes/No questions such as:

Is it a person?
Is it something which you use in the house?
Is it something that runs on electricity?
Is it something that I could put in my pocket?, etc.

If the panel have not discovered the item in 20 questions, they lose and the rest of the class wins.
5 The game continues as above through the other items on the list.
6 At the end count up who won most rounds, the panel or the class and declare the winner.

Exercises 2 and 3 These constructions may be new to students. Make sure they realise they can only be used when the subjects of both halves of the sentence are the same.

Classroom treatment These exercises could be done initially orally round the class, then each student could write the sentences as consolidation of the oral work.

Exercise 2 **Answers**

1 Not knowing the 'best buy' myself, I'll take your advice.
2 Having just bought a new wristwatch, I ought to get to my appointments on time now.
3 Not being a very technical person, he couldn't understand it.
4 Never having had a dishwasher, she won't miss it.
5 Having agreed to help with the party, I thought I'd better get there early.

Exercise 3   *When* could be used in the place of *while*

When could be used instead of *on*

On can't be used in 3b because *on* implies *at the moment when*

1 While doing everything we can to dispatch orders quickly, we can't work miracles!

2 Moving smoothly across any lawn it picks up all the leaves. *OR* It moves smoothly across the grass, picking up all the leaves.

3 On hearing the warning sound you must immediately switch off the machine.

4 While recommending 'Brand X', the manufacturers cannot of course insist on your using it.

5 While agreeing that/Though agreeing that *this* tin opener is quite good, I must say that *that* one is much easier to use.

Listening   This listening section and the follow-up discussion and written work aim to consolidate the grammar reviewed on pages 32 and 33.

Style of text: racy, energetic

Register: advertising language

Focus vocabulary

harassed: worried by repeated trouble

servicing: the repairing of a machine

📼 Tapescript

TUTOR:	Unit 5. Consumer Society. Look at page 33, Listening. Listen to this advertisement. It's the kind of thing you might hear on a commercial radio station.
1ST VOICE:	Calling all harassed businessmen! Do you you have to run off copies of reports, letters, leaflets, accounts at short notice? Do you need a quick copy of that letter and can't wait for someone to retype it for you? If so, then you're the sort of person who needs the new KOPI-ALL photocopier! Being the busy person you are, you'll wonder how you've ever managed without a photocopier like this. And having once used the KOPI-ALL machine, you'll never need to be harassed again.
MR JAMES:	KOPI-ALL's a wonderful machine. I can certainly recommend it. We've only had ours for a month, but already business is picking up and my secretaries wonder how they ever managed before. It's fast, it photocopies four different sizes of paper, it reduces and expands drawings or photos – and what's most amazing, it'll copy colour.
1ST VOICE:	So you see. No sooner had Mr James had a KOPI-ALL installed than his business showed signs of improvement.
2ND VOICE:	Remember. KOPI-ALL will save you time and money – and worry. And not only does it make photocopies – any other photocopier will do that – but it photocopies in different sizes, and in black and white or colour.
1ST VOICE:	And the cost? Incredible as it is, a KOPI-ALL could be yours for only £25 a month, with free installation and servicing. This offer lasts for a month from today. So the longer you wait, the more you could regret it.
2ND VOICE:	KOPI-ALL. It copies everything – perfectly.
TUTOR:	If you wish to listen to the advertisement again, rewind the tape.

Exercise 1   **Answers**

1 for photocopiers; 2 (harassed) businessmen; 3 very satisfied indeed; 4 photocopy four different sizes of paper, reduce and expand drawings and photos and copy colour; 5 £25 per month with free installation and servicing; 6 one month

Coursebook pp 34–35

Oral Interview Preparation Exercise 1 Dealing with the passages The second part of the Interview Paper requires students to read a short passage and then to say where it comes from, who it is spoken by, etc, and to comment on its content.

The passages, which could be in a range from very informal to very formal, written or spoken, serve mainly as a stimulus for discussion. One or more of the following types of comment can therefore validly be made by the candidate: agreeing or disagreeing with issues in a passage; relating any similar circumstances, events or situations; reacting on the emotional level; giving further information on any of the points contained in a passage.

Suggested answers

Passage a): Spoken language, fairly informal (use of short sentences, short forms *I'm, it's*; and idiomatic expressions such as *it cost a fortune*), possibly an excerpt from a TV documentary on the disabled. *Comment and discussion:* other uses of computers; other cases of disablement; the pros and cons of spending considerable amounts of money on disabled individuals.

Passage b): Neutral language, possibly journalistic, could be spoken or written, possibly an extract from a TV or radio documentary, or newspaper or magazine article. *Comment and discussion:* opinions on hippies and their beliefs, on John Lennon or the song *Imagine*, or candidate's recounting of personal knowledge of a hippy or similar community.

Passage c): Formal language, spoken or written (with use of nouns *introduction, legislation, access* in place of verbs), possibly excerpt from radio news or from a serious newspaper article. *Comment and discussion:* opinions on video nasties, on their influence, on the wisdom of government intervention; personal knowledge of these videos and/or their effects.

Exercise 2 Remember that for the reasons given in the General Introduction there is no test at the end of the three Units on the Interview Paper. To see an example of a full Interview Paper see Unit 15, Paper 5 in the Practice Exam at the end of the Course Book and the Interview Papers in *Longman Proficiency Practice Exams*.

Classroom treatment

1 Revise the expressions introduced at the beginning of the Unit that are used to ask for repetition and clarification, and to express assumptions and uncertainty.

2 Students could interview one another in pairs or discuss possible answers in pairs or groups before interviewing one another. Of course, the teacher can monitor student performance at this stage and give students feedback on how well they have done, though this could also be done by the student who is acting as the examiner.

Exercise 3 Game: Just a minute This is a very popular British radio game. In it a person is given a topic and then has to speak on it for one minute coherently and non-stop. If he doesn't manage, the other players challenge him and take over the topic. If this challenge isn't accepted by the referee, the original speaker continues with the topic and wins a point if he manages to keep speaking for the minute. As this game can be somewhat unnerving if played in an atmosphere of competition or shyness, it might be best to play it in groups for the first time rather than as a team game.

Object of the game To speak for one minute on a given topic without hesitating, digressing, repeating yourself or becoming incoherent, and to win as many points as possible.

Conduct of the game

1 Explain the rules of the game.
2 Divide the class into groups of four or five, and appoint one member of each group as referee.
3 Give each group a pile of topic cards with one topic on each (e.g. corporal punishment in schools, punk music, food, sport, pop stars). Students then take it in turns to take a card from the central pile, read it and then try to talk for a minute without giving the other students cause to challenge him or her.
4 If another student challenges correctly (e.g. for repetition, etc.) he or she can continue talking on the topic; if not, the original speaker continues. The student who is speaking at the end of the minute wins the point.
5 The game then continues with another student taking the next card from the topic pile and trying to talk for a minute.

N.B. The teacher should not interrupt the flow of the game to correct mistakes.
(See General Introduction for *Correction procedures.*)

UNIT 6 Science and Science Fiction

Aims of the Unit
1 To remind students of three reading skills: skimming, reading for detail and guessing the meaning of words from context.
2 To familiarise students with the multiple-choice testing technique.
3 To introduce students to three methods of looking at vocabulary: shades of meaning, vocabulary areas and collocation in preparation for Section A of the Reading Comprehension Paper.
4 Grammar: to review some uses of the Present Perfect, Simple Past and Past Perfect tenses.
5 To expand students' knowledge of vocabulary connected to the topic of *Science and Science Fiction.*

Coursebook pp 36–37

Exercise 1   This is a warm-up/lead-in activity intended to introduce the theme of the following text and of the Unit.

Classroom treatment As indicated in the Coursebook. The following could be used as discussion prompts if they are needed:
– Have you seen any of the big science fiction films, for example *Star Wars* or *The Empire Strikes Back*?
– Do you know the George Orwell novel *1984*? Do you consider that to be science fiction?
– What other science fiction writers do you know?, etc.

Exercise 2   **Background information** This extract is taken from the novel *2010: Odyssey Two* by Arthur C. Clarke. It is a sequel to the novel *2001: A Space Odyssey* which was written by the same author and made into a very successful film.
Note that the way Professor Chang speaks in the extract is often similar to the language of telegrams (telegraphese). This is because he is speaking over a radio and in a most urgent situation.

Style of text: dramatic, narrative

Register: neutral

Focus vocabulary
N.B. The focus vocabulary given below is the object of Exercise 5 on page 37 and should therefore not be taught before the extract is read in class.
a range: the distance at which one can see or hear
to fade: to (cause to) lose strength, colour, freshness, etc.
stunned: shocked into helplessness. This word collocates here with *silence* making a fixed phrase.
a tank: a large container for storing liquid or gas
seaweed: any of various (masses of) plants, especially dark green with long stems, growing in the sea

to crawl: to move slowly with the body close to the ground or floor, or on hands and knees

kelp: any of several kinds of large brown seaweed

to buckle: to (cause to) become bent or wavy, through heat, shock, pressure, etc.

to topple: to (cause to) become unsteady and fall down

Exercise 3   **Classroom treatment** Remind students of the need and reasons for reading for gist, then check their gist comprehension of the extract by asking them to answer these questions *without* reading the extract again.

Possible answers Dr Floyd is aboard the *Leonov* listening in to Chang's message. Dr Lee has died on Europa, and Professor Chang is on Europa relaying a radio message to the *Leonov*.

Exercise 4   This short multiple-choice comprehension exercise aims to get students to approach multiple-choice items correctly, i.e. by referring back to the text to read carefully amongst the details so as to be sure that one answer is correct and the other three wrong. This is achieved by the discussion method recommended in the Coursebook which forces students to justify their answers to one another by referring back to the text.

Classroom treatment

1 Each student individually marks what he thinks is the right answer.

2 As suggested in the Coursebook i.e. group discussion or pyramid discussion (see Introduction: Methods of conducting discussions).

N.B. The teacher should not give the students any indication of the correct answers at this stage so as to oblige them to find them confidently themselves.

3 Class discussion of correct answers with the teacher to confirm their correctness.

Answers

1 D; 2 C; 3 C; 4 C; 5 A.

Exercise 5   **Answers** See above in *Focus vocabulary*

Coursebook pp 38–39

Vocabulary in reading
Exercise 1
Differences
in meaning

This activity is designed to make students aware of the wide range of vocabulary concepts and of shades of meaning. Students even at this level often do not possess or recognise detailed vocabulary, although they need to. The three related word groups proposed are just examples of a very frequent phenomenon that cannot be treated more fully in a book of this length. But students should, by the end of the activity, see the value of this approach to vocabulary, and the teacher could usefully focus any future vocabulary work on this kind of approach when appropriate.

N.B. This activity is *not* intended to test students' knowledge of these words, but to guide them towards realising how fine the distinctions between words can be. Dictionaries should therefore be made available.

Classroom treatment As indicated in the Coursebook.

Answers

1 A boat can sink or capsize.

A building can topple.
A person can tumble.
Sales figures can slump.

N.B. Of course, other combinations are possible if extra words are added e.g. He slumped into the chair.

to sink: to (cause to) go down below a surface, out of sight, or to the bottom (of water)

to tumble: to fall suddenly or helplessly; roll over or down quickly or violently

to topple: to (cause to) become unsteady and fall down

to capsize: to turn over (especially of a boat or ship)

2 A signal can fade, dim, glimmer or flicker if it is a light, and fade or die away if it is a sound.
A light can fade, dim, glimmer, or flicker.
A candle can fade, dim, glimmer, or flicker.
A voice can fade or die away.
A colour can fade.

to fade: to (cause to) lose strength, colour, freshness, etc.

to dim: to (cause to) become dim i.e. not bright

to glimmer: to give a very faint, unsteady light

to die away: (especially of sound, wind, light) to fade and become less and less and cease

to flicker: to burn unsteadily; shine with an unsteady light

3 Water can trickle.
Mud can ooze.
A baby can crawl or creep.
A person can crawl, creep or stroll.
An insect can crawl.

to crawl: to move slowly with the body close to the ground or floor, or on hands and knees

to creep: to move slowly and quietly with the body close to the ground

to trickle: to flow in drops or in a thin stream

to ooze: to pass or flow slowly

to stroll: to walk, especially slowly, for pleasure

Exercise 2
Vocabulary areas The main purpose of this text is to suggest to students a second way of grouping vocabulary together i.e. word fields. For this reason not too much class time should be spent on comprehension work. Answering question 1 should be sufficient.

Style of text: narrative, slightly sensational

Register: neutral, scientific in parts

Answers

Space vocabulary: astronauts, Moon, lunar, space travel, space exploration, planet, rings of Saturn, Io, Europa, Ganymede, Callisto, space probes, spaceship.

Writing/Authorship vocabulary: fictional creation, novel, science fiction, writer, sequel, vocabulary, fiction, to publish, a copy, a synopsis, a word processor, a typewriter.

Adjectives of praise: brilliant, successful, breath-taking, spectacular.

Coursebook pp 40–41

Exercise 3
Collocation

This exercise aims to introduce students to word collocation, a feature of language which can play a large part in determining correct answers in Section A of the Reading Comprehension Paper. Collocation is something which students can look out for and remember in their general reading. They will need to have it brought to their attention, however, as a feature of language before they can do this. This passage has been included to show examples of collocation in use as well as to extend the space vocabulary area. For this reason not too much class time should be spent on comprehension work. Answering question 1 should be sufficient.

Style of text: descriptive. N.B. Note the American spelling and writing conventions in the following: *disk* (BrE *disc*), *traveled* (BrE *travelled*), *April 25* (BrE *on April 25th*), *March 3* (BrE *on March 3rd*), *June 13* (BrE *June 13th*).

Register: scientific

Classroom treatment

1 Find out what the students already know about Pioneer.
2 As indicated in the Coursebook. You might also include some discussion of collocation and see what examples students can think of in their own language. This will help them to see the importance of collocation.

Answers

1   It has gone further than any other man-made space craft.
     It has taken close-up images of Jupiter.
     It has made detailed observations of Jupiter's powerful radiation belts.
     It has discovered that Jupiter's sphere of magnetic influence extends to the orbit of Saturn.
     It has well exceeded its lifetime.

2   Earth, light, Sun, spacecraft, to cruise, Pluto, the solar system, solar particles, cosmic rays, gravity waves, force, Uranus, Neptune, to launch, Mars, Jupiter, radiation belts, a sphere of magnetic influence, orbit, Saturn, mission, dish antenna, outbound trajectory, elliptical.

4a) the signal *vanished/faded*: a *stunned* silence; a *school* of fish; a *good fund* of jokes; I couldn't think *straight*.

 b) the *far* side of the Moon; the *faintest hint* of a smile; to *conceal* his glee; a mere *pinpoint* of light.

Grammar

Students at this level may still be having problems distinguishing between the uses of the Present Perfect, the Simple Past and Past Perfect tenses. Use this review to remind students of the uses of these tenses and then take every opportunity from now on to focus students' attention on them if they continue to make mistakes. General rules for the use of these tenses are:

The Past Simple tense is used for actions or events which are seen by the speaker or writer to belong totally to the past, to be finished and complete.

The Present Perfect tenses are used for actions or events that either started in the past and continue in the present or that are seen by the speaker or writer to have some link with, influence or effect on the present.

The Past Perfect tenses are only used to stress that one past action or event happened before something else. It is not compulsory to use the Past Perfect tenses with two consecutive past actions e.g. both of the following are good English:

     After he had breakfast he went to the office.
     After he had had breakfast he went to the office.

The second sentence merely stresses that one action happened before the other.

Exercises 1, 2, 3   **Classroom treatment** We recommend you to ask the students to do all these exercises individually before discussing answers with the class as a whole.

Exercise 2   **Answers**

1 False; 2 False; 3 True; 4 True; 5 False; 6 False; 7 True; 8 False; 9 False; 10 True

Exercise 3   1 has delighted/delights; 2 had travelled; 3 has visited; 4 set foot; 5 have seen; 6 was launched; 7 was; 8 has stopped; 9 did it go/had it gone; 10 had/had had

Exercise 4   **Classroom treatment** The General Knowledge Quiz could be done as a team game as follows:

1 Students in groups of four or five devise their own True/False sentences.
2 These same groups then arrange themselves into teams and take it in turn to read out their sentences to the other groups. The first group to give the right answer gets a mark.
3 The game continues until all the teams have read out all their sentences, then the marks are added up and the team with the most marks is declared the winner.

Answers

1 True; 2 False; 3 False; 4 False; 5 False

Coursebook pp 42–43

Test Reading Comprehension   We recommend you get students to do the test in class under exam-like conditions and in the recommended time.

Answers

Section A: 1 D; 2 B; 3 D; 4 B; 5 B; 6 A; 7 D; 8 B; 9 C; 10 A; 11 D; 12 C; 13 B; 14 D; 15 A

Section B: 16 C; 17 B; 18 A; 19 D; 20 A

Suggested marking scheme   Section A: Score 1 mark for each correct item to give a possible maximum of 15 marks.

Section B: Score 2 marks for each correct item to give a possible maximum of 10 marks.

Possible total maximum for the whole test: 25 marks.

UNIT 7 The Energy Debate

Aims of the Unit
1 To familiarise students with different styles of written English.
2 To enable students to understand the reasons for varying styles.
3 To introduce students to the different kinds of expansion work that can form part of the Directed Writing Composition Exercise in the Composition Paper.
4 To provide students with language for approving or disapproving, as is frequently required in the Directed Writing Composition Exercise in the Composition Paper.
5 Grammar: to review various uses of modal verbs.
6 To expand students' knowledge of vocabulary connected to the topic of *The Energy Debate.*

Coursebook pp 44–45

Exercise 1   The photo, taken in a country in Western Europe in the 1980s, is intended to motivate thought and discussion on the topic of the Energy Debate.

Exercise 2   The letter on the left is an example of formal written English, whereas the one on the right is much more informal. Students may well be expected to recognise and produce different levels of formality in the Proficiency Exam. Various factors determine how formal a piece of language will be; the topic, the speaker or writer, the situation, the setting and the relationship between the speaker or writer and his audience. For example, a prime minister talking to another minister in his/her office about the budget is likely to employ fairly formal language. That same prime minister sitting at home on the same night and telling his wife/her husband about the same budget is likely to speak less formally, though not necessarily informally. Two students who are good friends are likely to use informal language to talk to one another about most subjects of mutual interest. Although there are no fixed rules about what level of formality has to be used in any given situation, breaking with the conventions can cause misunderstanding and even offence.

Classroom treatment

1 Ask each student to make notes in answer to the questions.
2 Students compare and discuss their answers in pairs.
3 Check the answers and lead into a discussion on why there are different levels of formality, when they need to be employed etc. as indicated above. N.B. If students have doubts about the existence or importance of degrees of formality point out to them in their own language two sentences of similar meaning but contrasting formality

e.g.	French	– Bonjour, Monsieur v. Salut, mon vieux
	Portuguese	– Bom dia, Senhor Gomes, como vai? v. Ola pá, estas bom?
	Italian	Buon giorno, signorina v. Ciao, Francesca

German — Wie geht es Ihnen? v. Wie geht's?
Greek — Herete v. Yiassou

– or two newspapers of different levels of formality as in Britain e.g. *The Times* v. *The Sun*.

Possible answers The message of the two letters is the same as regards the information it contains, but is not the same on the level of the relationship between the writer and the reader. The writer of the first letter treats his reader with an apparent show of respect, impersonally and somewhat coldly, whereas the second is much more direct and frank. The letters differ so much possibly because one claims to be an answer to a letter to *The Times* (a rather formal newspaper) and/or possibly because it was written by someone of a rather formal disposition, while the other is written for a different kind of audience by someone with a different view of himself/herself and his relationship with other people.

Exercise 3　**Classroom treatment** Encourage students to answer more fully than 'one is formal and one informal'. Ask them how they recognise this formality and informality in anticipation of Exercise **4** and also to give some examples.

Exercise 4　**Classroom treatment** As indicated in the Coursebook. This exercise is best done in pairs or groups before a general report back.

Answers

Formal written English examples:

1 I'm afraid . . . serious consideration.
However, it could surely not . . . kind of work.
No, Sir, I fear . . . advantage in.

2 as: as well as; however; nor; also

3 Passive: the bullock . . . be reintroduced
the proposal cannot be given . . .
it could surely not be called . . .

Conditional: if . . . you are seriously suggesting . . . the
proposal cannot be given . . .
it could surely not . . ./nor would anyone . . .

Introductory
phrases:　I'm afraid that . . .
I also have strong reservations as to . . .
I fear that . . .

4 ————

5 to reintroduce; contributing to; to return; prepared; a situation

6 non-pollutant; to permit savings

7 cannot; could surely not

Informal written English examples:

1 Paragraphs 4 and 5 contain shorter sentences. This letter as a whole contains five paragraphs compared with four in the other.

2 and; but; either

3 Active; we should start farming with bullock . . . progress?
Present tense: and call that progress

Introductory
phrases:　I'd like to know; apparently

Rhetorical
questions: Are you seriously suggesting . . . power again?
do you really think . . . progress?

who do you think you'd find?
How many fields . . . a day?
but to produce less . . . import more?
What's the sense in that?

4 ——————

5 to start again; good for; to make do again; willing

6 don't pollute; to save on

7 I'm; we'd; you'd; I'd; we'd; what's

Exercises 5 and 6 **Classroom treatment** We recommend you to get students to begin these exercises in class as they need guidance and help while doing it.

Possible answers

Formal

1 May I thank you for your letter/I would like to thank you for . . ./I am writing to thank you for . . .
2 I must apologise for not having written before/Please accept my apologies for not having written before.
3 I'm afraid I really can't agree . . ./I'm afraid I really don't agree . . ./I find it difficult to agree . . .
4 as . . ./because . . ./since . . .
5 I would be (extremely) pleased if you would/could come to visit . . ./I would very much like to invite you . . .
6 I look forward to hearing from you. I remain . . .

Informal

1 Thanks for/Thank you for . . .
2 (I'm) sorry not to have written before/Sorry I didn't write before . . .
3 I don't agree/I don't think . . .
4 (because) . . .
5 Why don't you come and visit my farm?/Would you like to come and visit my farm?
6 I hope to hear from you soon.

Exercise 7
Discussion **Classroom treatment** The following could be used as discussion prompts if they are needed:

– bicycles v. cars; walking v. public transport; stairs v. lifts; factory workers v. robots; sewing, knitting, gardening, etc. by hand v. with a machine.

These rather specific prompts could then lead into the discussion of more general issues such as employment; the quality of work; protection of the environment; health and drudgery and their relationship to the saving of energy.

Coursebook pp 46–47

Directed Writing A Directed Writing exercise is one of the three kinds of composition students may be asked to write in the Composition Paper. The four examples given on pages 46 and 47 are designed to familiarise students with possible formats for this part of the Composition Paper and to make them realise that these compositions require not only the expansion of given ideas but also, and very importantly, the correct use of tone, style and register.

Exercises 1–4 **Classroom treatment**

1 The teacher could go through the first exercise with the class as a whole to make sure they all understand what they have to do.

2 Exercises **2**, **3** and **4** could be done in groups.

3 Report back on exercises **2–4**.

N.B. It is *not* necessary for students to write the compositions.

Suggested answers

Exercise 1 Expansion work: a newspaper article
Style: this would depend on what kind of newspaper the journalist was working for. Students should make this point.
Tone: approving; praising; enthusiastic.

Exercise 2 Expansion work: a letter
Style: probably formal as the Director of the school is unknown to the writer.
Tone: angry; disapproving; determined; shocked

Exercise 3 Expansion work: interview or dialogue
Style: this would depend on the interviewer and on his/her newspaper and on Mrs Hepworth. They may choose to address one another either formally or neutrally.
Tone: Mrs Hepworth: angry; outspoken; fiery.
Interviewer: at the student's discretion, but in any case he/she must always respond appropriately to the tone employed by Mrs Hepworth and remain polite.

Exercise 4 Expansion work: the written version of the outline of a speech
Style: probably formal as the audience is widowed old ladies and the topic of the speech is somewhat formal. However, the speaker could choose a neutral register or even a more informal one if he thought it would be more appropriate and effective.
Tone: this would depend on the speaker; it could be objective and calm, it could be passionate, etc.

The Language of Approval and Disapproval The Directed Writing exercise in the Composition Paper often requires students to express approval or disapproval of particular situations. The language presented on page 47 of the Coursebook is designed to help them do this. The language of approval and disapproval can be expressed in varying degrees of formality, which students will have to be able to use appropriately. This is why they are asked to mark the expressions given in terms of their level of formality.

Exercises 1 and 2 **Classroom treatment** These activities could either be done individually by each student and then by a report back/discussion with the whole class, or they could be done with the class as a whole and accompanied by discussion. It may also be useful to ask students to try to say once again what seem to be the characteristics of the formal and informal expressions.

Exercise 1 **Answers** Some of the expressions are definitely formal, some definitely informal and others could be either formal or informal depending on the situations in which they occur.
1 F; 2 I; 3 I; 4 F; 5 F; 6 F; 7 F; 8 F; 9 F/I; 10 F/I; 11 F/I; 12 F/I; 13 F; 14 F/I; 15 F; 16 F/I; 17 I; 18 F/I

Exercise 2 Expressions of Approval: 2; 3; 5; 6; 8; 9; 11; 13; 16; 17; 18

Expressions of Disapproval: 1; 4; 7; 10; 12; 14; 15

Exercise 3
Vocabulary Building The aim of this exercise is to consolidate the approach to vocabulary areas introduced in Unit 6.

Classroom treatment After each student has complete his/her lists, ask students to compare lists or write up on the blackboard words that they suggest.

Possible answers

disappointed; appalled; shocked; disturbed; happy; glad; thrilled

Exercise 4
Collocation

The aim of this exercise is to consolidate the concept of collocation introduced in Unit 6.

Possible answers

completely/extremely disgusted; completely/extremely/greatly/highly/thoroughly/ very satisfied; absolutely/completely/thoroughly/utterly horrified; extremely/very upset; extremely/very pleased; thoroughly/absolutely delighted

Coursebook p 48

Listening

The aim of this section is to expose students to formal spoken English and also to get them to use it themselves in their own discussion.

Style of text: discursive, slightly polemical

Register: formal, current affairs

Focus vocabulary

running (adj.): (of money) spent or needed to keep something working
to overlook: to look at but not see; not notice; miss
astronomical: very large
to entertain: to be ready and willing to think about
utmost: of the greatest degree
to scar: to (cause to) be marked with a scar i.e. a mark of damage
to run the risk: to take chances/a chance

Exercises 1 and 2

The progression followed in these exercises is as follows:

Exercise 1 1: listening for gist and general information.
Exercise 1 2: listening for detailed information.
Exercise 2:   listening for language.

📼 Tapescript

TUTOR: Unit 7. The Energy Debate. Look at page 48. You're going to hear part of a serious radio programme in which two politicians discuss nuclear energy. Listen to it once and say what position each speaker holds on the subject. Ready?

MAN: The way to reduce imports is not to bring the bullock back into farming, but to build nuclear power stations. That way, there's no dependence on any foreign power for energy supplies.

WOMAN: I'm afraid that's far from being the case. You may not have to import the energy, but you do have to import uranium and also all the technology required to build and run a nuclear power plant.

MAN: That may be, but once a nuclear plant has been built, you don't need to go on importing technology, and actual running costs are low so we'd have more of the taxpayer's money available to finance, well, the social services, for example.

WOMAN: I think once again you're overlooking a very important point: the running costs of a nuclear plant may well be relatively low, but the initial capital expenditure is astronomical! It involves sums that our present-day economy certainly couldn't entertain, so the only way we could build a nuclear plant would be by international borrowing, and then how could we talk of being independent of any foreign power? No, to my mind, nuclear power means two things only – dependence and danger . . .

MAN: That, for me, is an example of muddled thinking. For so many people the main association of the word 'nuclear' is, well understandably, bombs and war. And people bring all these fears to any discussion of nuclear power, when in fact all nuclear plants have to conform to the strictest safety and security measures, and they have an excellent record of accident-free operation.

WOMAN: Perhaps they have, but the same can't be said for the disposal of nuclear waste, a factor you seem not to be considering . . .

MAN: As you well know, the utmost care is taken to dispose of waste, and once again our record has been a good one, which I'm afraid can't be said of other energy industries. We all know only too well how oil has polluted our seas and beaches and killed off marine life. We've watched coal mines scar our landscape and pollute our air, not to mention the diseases miners run the risk of catching. Of course, solar energy is a safe clean source of energy, but we're all well aware of how limited its applications are. In today's day and age I see little alternative to meeting our energy needs outside nuclear power.

WOMAN: Once again you seem to be closing your eyes to a vital issue: conservation. To my mind, conservation is the one thing that all those in favour of nuclear energy . . .

TUTOR: Now rewind the tape, listen to the discussion again and note the arguments expressed for and against nuclear energy.

TUTOR: And that's the end of Unit 7.

Suggested answers

Exercise 1   1 The man is in favour of the introduction of nuclear power; the woman is against it.
2 Arguments *for* nuclear energy:
 – no dependence on foreign power
 – low running costs
 – more taxpayer's money available for other things
 – excellent record of accident-free operation
 – no more dangerous than many other sources of energy
Arguments *against* nuclear energy:
 – extremely expensive to build and install, therefore would need to borrow from abroad, therefore increased dependence on foreign powers
 – danger of nuclear waste
 – possibility of conservation

Exercise 2   Group 1: – I'm afraid that's far from being the case.
 – I think once again you're overlooking a very important point.
 – That, for me, is an example of muddled thinking.
 – Perhaps they have, but the same can't be said for . . .
 – Once again you seem to be closing your eyes to a vital issue.
Group 2: 1 to run; 2 to overlook; 3 astronomical; 4 to entertain; 5 to my mind; 6 muddled; 7 a factor; 8 utmost; 9 to scar; 10 to run the risk of

Exercise 3
Role play   Role plays may form part of the Proficiency Interview Paper. Here it is important to encourage students to use as much of the language they heard on tape as possible.

Exercise 4   **Classroom treatment** To try to ensure that everyone has something to say during
Discussion   the discussion, you could ask students to jot down on a piece of paper any ideas

they have for viable solutions before beginning the discussion. (Give them about 5 minutes.) The following could be used as discussion prompts if they are needed:

– How realistic is conservation? What real difference would it make?
– Can solar energy make any significant contribution?
– What about wind, wave and geothermal energy?

Coursebook p 49

Style The purpose of this activity is to bring together the two strands developed in this Unit i.e. style and the language of approval and disapproval. This is a consolidation task.

Exercises 1 and 2 Exercise 2 is a blank-filling exercise similar to that to be found in Section A of the Use of English Paper. These exercises always require gist understanding before detailed understanding, and this is why Exercise 1 has been included in the Coursebook.

Answers

1 utmost; 2 ahead; 3 plant; 4 only; 5 has; 6 or; 7 Yet; 8 expose; 9 wish/have; 10 but; 11 sincerely; 12 them/it
1 congratulations; 2 on; 3 taken/made; 4 last; 5 to; 6 How; 7 that; 8 finally; 9 in; 10 with

Coursebook pp 49–50

Grammar These modal constructions are occasionally tested in Section A of the Use of English Paper. They also form part of rather more formal styles of English and are therefore useful to students for their composition work.

Classroom treatment The three exercises could be done in small groups and then the answers checked with the class as a whole.

Answers

Exercise 1
1 Everyone has an obligation/is under an obligation to save energy.
2 There is no necessity (for us) to build more power plants.
3 There is a possibility of us/of our being able to meet our energy requirements.
4 The capacity of coal to cause fatal diseases is often overlooked.
5 There is a probability that oil will run out soon in certain producer countries.

Exercise 2
1 There must be a solution.
2 There must have been/should have been/ought to have been an investigation.
3 there may (well) be/there might be . . .
4 there may/might/should/could be . . .
5 There should be/ought to be . . .
6 there could possibly be . . .
7 There should have been/ought to have been . . .
8 There must be . . .
9 There could/might/may (well) be . . .
10 There should have been/ought to have been . . .

Exercise 3 1 He was sorry not to be able to see them.
2 He was afraid of having to show his passport.
3 He was angry at not being able to solve the problem.
4 It's a pity (for us) to have had to leave so soon.
5 Not being able to help him, they've sent him to the Tourist Office.
6 He regretted not having been able to go.

Coursebook p 51

Homework exercises Students must be encouraged to complete the Homework exercises within the recommended time. Further, at this stage, they should hand in plans and Compositions.

Exercise 1 Possible phrases of 'angry protest' that students might use:
– I feel compelled to express considerable consternation at . . .
– It was with the utmost dismay that I heard . . .
– I find I have no choice but to register my disgust at . . .
– I would like to express my strong disapproval of . . .

Test Composition We recommend you to get students to do the test in class under exam-like conditions and in the recommended time.

Answers The compositions written on this title will vary with each student. Make sure, however, that their content is always relevant to the title and also includes all the points mentioned in the title.

Suggested marking scheme As Test for Unit 2. See page 28 of this Teacher's Guide.

UNIT 8 The Technological Revolution

PAPER 3: **USE OF ENGLISH**

Aims of the Unit
1 To prepare students for transformation exercises of the kind found in Section A of the Use of English Paper.
2 To prepare students for the open-ended comprehension questions found in Section B of the Use of English Paper.
3 Grammar: to review the use of certain Passive constructions.
4 To expand students' knowledge of vocabulary connected to the topic of *The Technological Revolution*.

Coursebook pp 52–53

Exercise 1 This exercise is intended as a warm-up to the topic of the Unit. As such it should not take up more than 5–10 minutes of class time.

Classroom treatment The following could be used as discussion prompts if they are needed:
– Have you ever heard of the Compact Disc?
– What do you know about it?
– What are the disadvantages of today's records?
– Are cassettes any better than records? Why?/Why not?
– How would the ideal record work?

Exercise 2 **Background information** This article was taken from *Which?*, a British consumers' protection magazine.

Style of text: factual, down to earth, simple

Register: neutral, slightly technical

Focus vocabulary
N.B. Students have to work out the meaning of the focus vocabulary in Exercise **3** on page 53, so do not teach it before reading the text in class.

to launch: to put on the market
to go over to: to change to
currently: at present
around: in existence
tough luck: bad luck; it's a great pity
to be after something: to want; to be looking for
esoteric: (of knowledge, interests, etc.) limited to a small circle of people
to pop: to put quickly and lightly
fiddly: awkward
setting-up: preparation for use
to jar: to bump or knock
tricky: difficult to handle or deal with

Cultural information

Beethoven's Fifth: Beethoven's Fifth Symphony
James Last: the leader of a band which plays popular music
Status Quo: a well-known British heavy-rock group

Classroom treatment to give students a reason for reading this article we suggest you ask them to read it to explain the subtitle 'A sound revolution?'.

Answer The subtitle is a play on the word *sound* = a) something you hear and b) sound investment and sound sense; i.e. will it be wise to invest in this new technology?

Exercise 3   **Answers** See above under *Focus vocabulary*

Exercise 4   The purpose of dividing up the comprehension work in this way ('Jigsaw reading',
Jigsaw reading   see p 30 of TG) is to give students added motivation to find the correct answers, to bring about communicative oral work as the students will have to tell one another their answers and to give students practice in the kind of 'structural communication exercise' that they may meet in Part Three of the Interview Paper.

Classroom treatment Although this exercise is not in preparation for a summary or composition, make sure that students are taking notes correctly i.e. only writing down the essential and changing the wording of the original text if this allows their notes to be more succinct. When the students reach the stage of telling one another their answers, make sure this stage is conducted as conversationally as possible i.e. don't let students simply read one another's answers or just read out their answers to one another.

Answers

Student A questions:
1 A compact disc is one that is played by laser beam.
2 Between £450–£650.
3 50% classical music plus some rock, jazz and pop.
4 It is about as easy as playing a cassette.

Student B questions:
1 Easy to set up, simple, compact, durable, easy to clean, adaptable.
2 Expensive, limited range of music available, shows up imperfections in recording, sound range not fully exploitable.
3 Not known as yet.
4 Probably here to stay, will develop.

Coursebook pp 54–55

Grammar   This section looks at some special uses of the Passive because students at this level must already have mastered more basic uses and because these particular uses could be tested in Section A of the Use of English Paper. They will also be useful for composition and comprehension work.

N.B. Although the Passive can be used in all tenses with Simple forms of verbs, it is extremely rare, if not impossible, with certain Continuous forms e.g. *it has been being written for 3 years* (Present Perfect Continuous); *it will have been being built for 6 years next spring* (Future Perfect Continuous); *the translation is going to be printed next week* ('going to' Future Continuous); *the new president will be being elected this time next week* ('will' Future Continuous); *the work had been being done for a long time* (Past Perfect Continuous). Such forms would rarely be used.

Exercises 1 and 2   **Classroom treatment** Ask students to write the answers to these exercises individually or in pairs before checking their answers with the class as a whole.

Answers

Exercise 1
1 Thousands of CD machines have been sold since 1983.
2 The concert tonight is being conducted by a famous composer.
3 That should have been discovered a long time ago.
4 The new video system was being demonstrated when I went there yesterday.
5 A solution might be found to the problem soon.

Exercise 2
1 You are to be/must be congratulated on passing your driving test.
2 He doesn't seem to mind being criticised.
3 Their house is being let, not sold. /Their house is to be let, not sold.
4 She didn't see her handbag (being) stolen.
5 You aren't to blame/to be blamed for what happened.
6 I didn't see the girl (being) knocked off her bicycle.
7 The manager was nowhere/wasn't anywhere to be found./The manager couldn't be found anywhere.
8 I don't want to be disturbed.
9 I didn't actually hear the news (being) announced.
10 He hates being asked about his past.

Vocabulary   The nouns presented on page 55 of the Coursebook are formed from phrasal verbs. They are often tested in Section A of the Use of English Paper in the way shown in Exercise 3. There are many of these nouns, but in this Unit we can only present a few. We therefore recommend you to point others out to students when they arise elsewhere, in comprehension, composition or discussion work.

Exercise 1   **Answers**

a)
Output at the factory increased 50% last year.
The *outcome* of the meeting was most unexpected.
She owes her success to the *upbringing* her parents gave her.
Right at the *outset* I must say this information is confidential.
The *upkeep* of the cathedral is very expensive.
There has been another *outbreak* of fighting on the border.
Our initial *outlay* (to start the business) was £5,000.
The *onset* of the disease is marked by a fit of coughing.
Suddenly there was an *outburst* of laughter from the next room

Other similar nouns: *inflow, inset, outlet, outcast, uplift, uptake,* etc.

b)
Let me give you a *rundown* of what the manager said.
One *drawback* of the scheme is the very high cost.
She gave the boy a *telling-off* for being so naughty.
That young girl wears far too much *make-up* for her age.
I'm sorry we're late, but we had a *breakdown* on the way here.
The impressionist did a *take-off* of the Prime Minister.
It was a major *breakthrough* in the field of telecommunications.
After what I had been led to expect, the concert was a *letdown*.
He said he was poor, but his new shoes were a *giveaway*.
There was a *break-in* at the office, but nothing was stolen.

Other similar nouns: *break-out, break-up, let-up, hold-all, hold-up, knock-out, knock-up,* etc.

Exercise 2
Game: Make up a story

Object of the game To give students an opportunity to use the nouns formed from phrasal verbs in speech and writing.

Conduct of the game

1 Divide the class into groups of 4.
2 Tell each group to write on a piece of paper any four of the nouns that are formed from phrasal verbs.
3 Each group exchanges their piece of paper with another group.
4 Each group makes up and writes a story which incorporates the four nouns on their piece of paper. N.B. These stories can be as likely or unlikely, serious or ridiculous as students choose!
5 Students re-form groups so that each new group contains one member of each of the old groups.
6 In groups the students tell one another the stories they have invented.

Exercise 3

This kind of transformation exercise is a regular feature of Section A of the Use of English Paper. When forming the new sentences students must remember that they *cannot* alter the word given in brackets in any way at all. This may mean that the new sentence has a completely different grammatical construction from the original one. What is important is that the meaning of the new and the original sentence must be exactly the same.

Classroom treatment

1 Do this exercise with the class as a whole to provide guidance. Don't allow students to write at this stage.
2 Students write their answers.
3 Pair checking of answers.

Answers

1 The boy's upbringing cost them a lot of money.
2 The average income in that country is about £1,000 a year.
3 The outcome of the long discussions was that nothing was done at all.
4 There were break-ins in three houses in our street last week.
5 The upkeep of this big house is becoming very expensive.
6 They gave us a detailed rundown of what had happened.
7 The restaurant was such a letdown that we never went back.
8 At the outbreak of the war many people tried to escape across the border.
9 The firm's initial outlay on the project was £15,000.
10 Her distinctive handwriting was her giveaway in the end. *OR* In the end, the giveaway was her distinctive writing.

Coursebook pp 56–57

Answering questions on a passage

As stated in the Coursebook these are the kinds of exercise found in Section B of the Use of English Paper. Students must learn to answer these questions accurately; weak answers tend not so much to be wrong as to supply too much information, a large percentage of which is irrelevant to the question. The kind of reading required by this kind of exercise is reading for detail and it might therefore be useful for students to underline those parts of the passage which contain the right answers.

Style of text: detailed, factual, very slightly sensational

Register: neutral

Focus vocabulary

Big Brother: a government leader or department which has too much power and allows no freedom

trivial: of little worth or importance
to keep tabs on: to watch closely
a filing cabinet: a piece of office furniture with drawers, for storing papers in

Cultural information:

Big Brother: this was a character created by George Orwell in his novel *1984*
Vehicle Licensing Department: this is a British government department in charge of
making sure that all vehicles have a licence and are taxed

Exercise 1 **Suggested answer** The article is about the increasing invasion of privacy in today's world caused by the computerisation of personal and business information and about the need to have safeguards against this invasion.

Exercise 2 **Classroom treatment** We recommend you to do this exercise orally initially with the class as a whole, and then to ask each student to write the answers. The aim here is to give students as much guidance as possible.

Suggested answers

4 essentially unimportant
5 unusual, out of the average way of spending money
6 to watch closely, make a careful note of
7 where files used to be stored, now out-of-date due to computers
8 became available to, came into the possession of
9 given permission for afterwards
10 met, fulfilled, kept to

Exercise 3 **Classroom treatment** As for Exercise 2.

Answers

4 library books borrowed; credit card spending patterns; changes of address; health; income; social security positions; details of property, car, job, etc.
5 because these people have in one way or another brought themselves to the attention of the authorities
6 to prevent financial damage
7 to establish the principles which should govern data protection
8 what is kept, why, for how long, for whose benefit, and for what purpose

Homework exercise Tell students to make notes before doing the summary and to hand the notes into you together with the summary.

Coursebook pp 58–59

Test Use of English We recommend you to get students to do the test in class under exam-like conditions and in the recommended time.

Answers

Section A 1 a) Only when you have read the report in detail will you be able to find the answers.
b) In spite of the fact that the technological revolution is opening up a whole new world, many people are worried by it.
c) He was annoyed at having to go back to his office in the evening.
d) So confused and worried did the boy become that he left home.
e) Never having seen or heard a compact disc, I can't comment on it.
f) On hearing the telephone ring, I answered it immediately.

g) I was very interested by/in the article about data protection.

h) The claims made by the manufacturers are being challenged by the record companies.

i) I didn't see the new computer being demonstrated while I was there.

j) There is a great deal to be done before we move house.

2 a) Wherever she goes, she always makes her presence felt.

b) There must be a solution to this problem.

c) It's not/hardly worth considering the other theories./The other theories aren't worth considering.

d) He works much more carefully these days.

e) We have no choice but to wait and see what happens.

f) I apologise for not writing/having written to you last month.

g) There's a possibility that they've got lost/of their having got lost.

h) Our outlay on this project has been considerable.

i) The comedian did a take-off of the Prime Minister in his stage act.

j) I would like to make a strong complaint about the play which was performed at your theatre last week.

Section B 3 N.B. The wording of these answers can vary but the information must be the same.

a) Its traditional way of life gave way to a new one.

b) Because it was disturbed by no mechanical noise.

c) Hands that touched and cared for the crops.

d) Because the horse was all-powerful.

e) As far as we could go.

f) Noise, greater travel, more visitors, the death of animals, illness or death amongst the old.

g) Those who were the first victims in the name of change.

h) Because in those days he measured everything with measures taken from the only world with which he was familiar.

i) Because there were few of them.

j) Because they preferred to walk and found these services extremely expensive.

k) The madness of modern life.

l) Main points only:
   – more people came and went
   – animals and people suffered or died
   – speed and noise
   – the break-up of the village and its age-old way of life

Suggested marking scheme

Section A

Exercise 1: Score 2 marks for each completely correct sentence, giving a possible maximum of 20 marks.

Exercise 2: Score 2 marks for each completely correct sentence, giving a possible maximum of 20 marks.

Section B

a)–k): Score a maximum of 2 marks for each of these answers to give a possible maximum of 22 marks.

Summary: Score 2 marks for the inclusion of each of the main points (see above) to give a total of 8 points for content. Then give an impression mark out of 10 for good English. This gives a possible maximum of 18 for the summary.

Total possible score for the whole test: 80 marks.

UNIT 9 Personal Experiences

PAPER 4: **LISTENING COMPREHENSION**

Aims of the Unit
1 To give further practice in predicting the content of listening comprehension pieces by careful reading of questions and tasksheets.
2 To give students practice in listening for gist, detailed information, feelings, attitudes, style and register.
3 To review grammar and vocabulary related to Reported Speech.
4 To expand students' knowledge of vocabulary connected to the topic of *Personal Experiences*.

Coursebook pp 60–61

Exercise 1 **Style of text:** anecdotal, narrative

Register: neutral

Focus vocabulary

a hall: a large room in which meetings, dances, etc. can be held
rasping: sounding rough and annoying
to hiss: to say in a sharp whisper
to slump: to sink down; fall heavily or in a heap

Tapescript

TUTOR: Unit 9. Personal Experiences. Look at page 60, Exercise 1. Listen to this short anecdote, and then answer the questions. Ready?

MAN: I was at one of those 'Music and Words' evenings at our local hall. You know, an evening of songs and poetry readings by local amateurs. There was a woman on the stage reading a poem. She had such a rasping voice that I turned to the man sitting next to me and, in a whisper, commented on it. He looked at me rather frostily and whispered back: 'That's my wife.' Not knowing quite what to do, and beginning to blush, I muttered: 'Oh, I didn't really mean her voice: I meant the poem she's reading.' He looked at me again and hissed: 'I wrote it.' I slumped down in my seat and hid my face. It was as near as I could get to disappearing through a hole in the floor!

Answers

1 in a hall; 2 reading a poem on a stage; 3 the woman's husband; 4 What a dreadful voice/awful voice she's got, hasn't she?/etc.; 5 He was embarrassed; 6 by trying to say that he was referring to the poem and not to the woman's voice; 7 he told the speaker he'd written the poem; angrily; sharply; 8 acutely embarrassed because he'd put his foot in it twice.

Exercise 2 This exercise focuses on encouraging students to predict the content of listening comprehensions, thus continuing the work started in Unit 4.

Style of text: conversational, anecdotal

Register: neutral

Focus vocabulary

baffled: confused
Ladies' Room: a women's lavatory in e.g. a hotel

🔲 Tapescript

TUTOR: Look at page 61, Exercise 3. Listen and answer the multiple-choice questions. Ready?

WOMAN: The situation I'm going to tell you about is one in which I could have dropped tons of bricks – and probably did!

A few years ago – I'd been a reporter on a national magazine for about two years, I think – I was invited along to one of those big parties in aid of charity. You know the kind – the sort of party where everyone is a celebrity, a 'famous name'. Well, I found myself in conversation with a man who'd been introduced to me, but I hadn't listened to the name. His face was familiar, but the name just wouldn't come. It was exasperating.

Anyway, we chatted amicably for twenty minutes or so. He seemed to know my name, asked how things were on the magazine, (and) even asked after my family; although how he knew about my work and my family, I just couldn't think. In return, as you do in polite conversation, I asked him what he did, how his career was going, how his wife was, and so on. All his answers were pretty vague, I thought. I was intrigued to find that he travelled a lot, and asked him if he took his wife when he travelled. On being told that they often travelled separately in Britain, but usually travelled abroad together, 'as I must know', I began to feel somewhat baffled, and also felt that I should know who he was. With a somewhat uncomfortable feeling, and a politely whispered 'It was very nice to meet you', I managed to extricate myself and made for the Ladies' Room.

It wasn't until after I reached the haven of the Ladies' Room and closed the door on the buzz of the party that the realisation dawned – I'd been speaking to the Duke of Edinburgh, and had actually asked him how his career was going! and how his wife (the Queen!) was! And of course he knew me! I had had the great fortune to interview him briefly for an article in my first year on the magazine. I could have died! – I didn't, of course. Instead, I collected my coat and slunk away, extremely flushed.

TUTOR: To listen to the anecdote again, rewind the tape.

Exercise 3   Answers
1 C; 2 A; 3 C; 4 D

Exercise 5   Style of text: conversational

Register: neutral

Focus vocabulary

to shatter: to break suddenly into small pieces; to damage badly; ruin; wreck
adrift: not fastened, and driven about by the sea or the wind; out of control; loose
to steer clear: to keep away from; to avoid
a gale: a weather condition in which strong winds blow

🔲 Tapescript

TUTOR: Look at page 61, Exercise 5. You're going to hear an extract from a radio programme about disasters and how people cope with them. Listen and answer the multiple-choice questions.

NARRATOR: . . . so disasters can in fact be major, or quite minor events in people's lives. It all depends how the people involved regard them.

For six years John Noakes had planned the voyage that would take him, his wife Vicky and their 14-metre boat halfway round the world, down into the Caribbean and the paradise island of Antigua.

In September '82, ten weeks out to sea, a freak storm blew up, and in a force 9 gale the Noakes' boat was shattered by a 20-metre wave that left the couple adrift for a day and a half off Spain.

The storm claimed 22 lives, but John and Vicky survived to be picked up by a passing tanker.

Back in England, John found it very difficult to steer clear of thoughts of sun-soaked West Indian islands.

'It's so depressing,' he moaned, staring out of his office window. 'But we're going back to sea. The first thing my wife said after the tanker had picked us up was, "We'll get the boat repaired, and set off again".' I thought 'Good grief – what have I married?'

Asked about the experience of being shipwrecked, John said: 'I kept thinking that if we'd set off two days later, we would have missed the storm. But at the time, no one expected a hurricane-force gale. We were just told to anticipate strong winds.

'Shortly before we were knocked down, I went up on deck and saw the biggest wave I'd ever seen. It was moving in slow motion and as a piece of power it was really quite beautiful. There was no time to be terrified. I just got back down below, and it was all over in a flash. I think we were lifted to the crest of the wave, then ran out of water, so the boat toppled down, with the wave crashing over us.'

TUTOR: To listen to the extract again, rewind the tape.

Answers

1 D; 2 B; 3 C; 4 D

Coursebook pp 62–63

Grammar This section on Reported Speech does not attempt to look at points such as the sequence of tenses, how to make indirect questions, negative commands, etc. By this stage students should have mastered these. The section looks instead at *Reported Speech* from the point of view of style with regard both to the formality of language and choice of vocabulary. This is in order to make students' language more precise and better adapted to particular situations i.e. appropriate. Students at Proficiency level frequently still have difficulty in expressing themselves appropriately in more formal situations and in informal ones. Several of the grammatical constructions focused on in this section may also be tested in Section A of the Use of English Paper. It could be useful to refer students back to the section in Unit 7 on formal and informal language before doing these exercises.

Style of text: impersonal

Register: neutral

Tapescript

TUTOR: Look at page 62 and listen.
You're going to hear a radio news item. Ready?

NEWSREADER: The time is 9 o'clock and here is the news. Figures published today indicate for the first time in six months that there has been a noticeable improvement in the country's economic situation. Speaking at the headquarters of the National Economic Council, a spokesman declared that the figures were very good news indeed for industry and for the rest of the country. When asked about the possibility of lower bank rates to help borrowing, however, he replied that it was far too early to tell, although he doubted whether the figures would force any such changes just yet. The spokesman added that the Council would be making a fuller statement when the figures had been analysed in detail.

TUTOR: If you wish to hear the news item again, rewind the tape.

Possible answers

1 The country's present economic situation. 2 Yes, it was formal. Some examples are: Figures published today . . . ; there has been a notable improvement in the country's economic situation; Speaking at the headquarters . . . a spokesman declared . . . ; When asked about the possibility . . . ; although he doubted whether the figures would force any changes just yet; the Council would be making a fuller statement when the figures had been analysed in detail.

Exercise 1   Answers

Speaking at the headquarters of the National Economic Council, a spokesman declared that the figures were very good news indeed for industry and for the rest of the country.
When asked about the possibility of lower bank rates to help borrowing, however, he replied that it was far too early to tell, although he doubted whether the figures would force any such changes just yet.

Exercise 2   First interview:

Style of text: direct, interview-like

Register: neutral

Focus vocabulary
infuriated: extremely angry

Second interview:

Style of text: impersonal, factual

Register: neutral

Focus vocabulary
to derail: to (cause to) run off the rails
a casualty: a person hurt in an accident

Third interview:

Style of text: factual

Register: neutral

Focus vocabulary
to collide: to meet and strike (together) violently
shaken: upset
faulty: (especially of machines, apparatus, etc.) having faults

Classroom treatment Instead of the classroom treatment indicated in the Coursebook, students could note down the answers after each interview, then compare them with a partner and finally with the class as a whole.

📼 Tapescript

TUTOR:	Look at page 62, Exercise 2. You're going to hear three interviews. Listen and report what was said.
	The first is with Cliff Priestley at his London flat.
INTERVIEWER:	Cliff, you're said to be one of the richest pop stars in the country, and there are rumours that you're leaving for the USA. Can you comment on that?
CLIFF:	No, I'm definitely not leaving. And, to be honest, I'm infuriated by accusations like that.
INTER.:	Infuriated?
CLIFF:	Yes. Basically, I'm being accused of not wanting to pay taxes, aren't I?
INTER.:	Well, I don't know. But how do you think these rumours started?
CLIFF:	I assume someone misunderstood the announcement about my forthcoming tour of the States. I'm very patriotic, and although obviously I pay a lot of Income Tax, I certainly don't want to leave this country to go and live in the States.
INTER.:	So what do you think of certain other artists and groups in the pop business who have left for the States? To live there permanently, I mean?
CLIFF:	I'm concerned that people who've had some success feel obliged to leave for tax reasons – but I don't agree with them.
TUTOR:	The second interview is with a spokesman for British Rail about a goods train which was derailed earlier today.
INTER.:	Can you give us any more information about the derailment?
SPOKESMAN:	No, I'm sorry I can't. We're mystified. It's the third on this stretch of line in the past month.
INTER.:	So is there any connection between this and the previous two, do you think?
SPOKESMAN:	It's possible. There could be. But we've found no evidence as yet to prove any connection.
INTER.:	I presume you know the causes of the previous two?
SPOKESMAN:	Yes. On the previous two occasions, the derailments were caused by large stones which had been thrown onto the line from a bridge. There's no evidence that this happened here.
INTER.:	Were there any casualties?
SPOKESMAN:	No, no one was hurt. And the line was only closed for twelve hours. It's open again now.
TUTOR:	And the third interview is with a policeman at the scene of an accident.
INTER.:	Sergeant, I wonder if you can tell me what happened?
POLICE SERGEANT:	Well, we're not quite sure at the moment. All we know is that three cars collided at the traffic lights here, and that all the occupants of the three cars have been taken to hospital for treatment.
INTER.:	Are any of them badly injured?
SERGEANT:	No, none. I believe they're all badly shaken.
INTER.:	Have you taken any statements yet?
SERGEANT:	No, not yet. We shall be interviewing them later. In the meantime, we want to get the road cleared.
INTER.:	And you've no way of knowing how the accident happened?
SERGEANT:	No. Nothing certain. The lights were reported to be faulty earlier today, so they may have stopped working. In which case, as you'll know, it's every man for himself. All three may have thought it was safe to cross. But at the moment we just don't know.
TUTOR:	Now rewind the tape, listen to the three interviews again and extract the main points from each in order to write news items.

Answers There can be no fixed answers for this exercise. Accept all answers which seem appropriate.

Exercise 3 **Classroom treatment** It may be necessary to play the tape a number of times to help students do this exercise and also to pause the tape after an answer has been given to allow them time to write notes.

Suggested answers

First interview: Cliff Priestley *not* leaving country. Angry at accusation. Is going to States on tour, not to live so as to avoid paying taxes. Too patriotic to do such a thing. Concerned that some people feel obliged to leave country but doesn't agree with them.

Second interview: Spokesman for British Rail speaks of derailment; third on same line in month; cause as yet unknown, but not result of stone throwing as others were; no casualties; line closed for 12 hours and now open again.

Third interview: Policeman talks of accident in which 3 cars collided; all occupants taken to hospital, shaken but not badly hurt; cause of accident unknown; no statements taken as yet; traffic lights had been reported faulty earlier in the day.

Exercise 4 **Classroom treatment** It would be best if students wrote these passages out in Reported Speech before reporting their answers to the class as a whole. In this way each student can appreciate the problems involved.

Possible answers

1 John asked Mary why they were/had been so disappointed and Mary said that when they (had) booked the tickets they (had) thought the seats were in the front row. John enquired if she hadn't asked at the box office and Mary said (that) she hadn't.

2 The judge enquired where the witness had been on the night of the 13th. (To which) the witness stated/replied/declared that he didn't know and couldn't remember. The judge then enquired whether he had tried to remember. (To which) the witness stated/replied/declared that he had of course but that he had no recollection of that night.

Exercise 5 **Answers**

Some other verbs that introduce Reported Speech are: *swear, beg, implore, recommend, invite, encourage, deny, order.* There are many others and students will probably come up with a range of them.

1 She advised me to go and ask the/that man.
   or She advised me (that) I (should) go and ask that man.
2 She warned the boy not to touch the hot iron.
3 He thanked her very much for helping him.
4 In court the man admitted (to) committing the robbery.
5 He encouraged them to eat it and told them they'd enjoy it.

Vocabulary **Classroom treatment**
Exercise 1 1 Give students time to read through the whole passage.
2 Let them think for a few minutes about the meanings of these verbs.
3 General class discussion of their meaning.

Answers

snapped implies irritation; *bawled* implies anger and noise; *muttered* implies complaint; *groaned* implies resigned complaint. There are many verbs which can show the mood or attitude of speakers and students will probably come up with a range of them. The following are just a few of them: *grumble, yell, whine, sneer, explain, moan, roar.*

Coursebook pp 64–65

Exercise 2 1 **Classroom treatment** This exercise is best done in pairs. The more doubt and discussion there is about each face the better as this will oblige the students to use the adjectives in the box in their discussion.

Possible answers

1 pleased or delighted; 2 mystified, confused, baffled; 3 bored, fed-up, depressed; 4 interested, fascinated, intrigued; 5 frightened; 6 annoyed, angry, indignant; /terrified; 7 surprised; 8 embarrassed; 9 disappointed

2 and 3 **Classroom treatment** Students may need a few minutes' thinking time to recall embarrassing/frightening/humiliating/exciting things or moments in their lives. Allow them all 2 or 3 minutes' silence before they begin to work in pairs or groups.

Homework exercises The time for this homework should be divided as follows: Ex.s **1** and **2** = 30 minutes; Ex. **3** = 1 hour, which includes planning, writing and checking the composition. Students should be asked to hand in the plan along with the composition.

Answers

Exercise 1 1 I must congratulate you on drawing up/having drawn up some excellent plans.
2 On being told about the robbery, the manager confessed to being astounded.
3 She was thoroughly embarrassed by the whole proceedings.
4 He advised him/her/me to go and speak to his/her/my bank manager.
5 He told us that he would have been here/there for twenty years by next/the following January.
6 They were so concerned about their son that they took him to a specialist.
7 Not being able to get through to the police, she ran next door for help.
8 Having to get up especially early, I set my alarm carefully.
9 I must apologise for not being able/not having been able to come to the meeting.
10 I was very irritated by the way he kept clicking his fingers.

Exercise 2 1 concerned/worried; 2 wondered; 3 being; 4 would; 5 puzzled/baffled/staggered; 6 annoyed/irritated; 7 asked; 8 going/planning; 9 way; 10 off; 11 thought; 12 having; 13 talking; 14 could/should/might; 15 revolutionary/original/brilliant

Coursebook pp 66–67

Test Listening Comprehension We recommend you to get students to do the test under exam-like conditions. Students should write their answers on a piece of paper.

📼 Tapescript

TUTOR: Unit 9. Listening Comprehension Test. Look at page 66. Questions 1–5. Read the five multiple-choice questions and then listen to an anecdote. But first read the questions.*

Now listen and answer the multiple-choice questions. Ready?

MAN: I think the most – the weirdest experience I've ever had was about ten years ago. No, 'weirdest' is not really the right word. 'Baffling'? 'Staggering'? 'Terrifying'? All those things, but . . . Well, let me tell you what happened.
I was driving home at about nine late one evening from doing some business in the north. It was a typical late November night. Very cold, with occasional patches of mist,

but generally quite a clear night. I was about two miles from the village where we live when I spotted a hitchhiker about 200 metres ahead on my side of the road. I was going to drive on past, because I never stop for hitchhikers – especially after that terrible mugging case a few years ago. But when I got closer, I realised that it was a man from our village – in fact, an acquaintance of ours: his wife was friendly with my wife, although I didn't know him at all well, apart from saying 'Good morning' occasionally. And I knew his name was John. But that's all.

Anyway, I stopped and he got in. He told me that his car had broken down outside Winchester – he'd also been on his way back from business. He'd left his car at a garage and had got a lift the 20 miles to the point where I had picked him up. That was all he said, as far as I remember, and I didn't press him further.

I dropped him at the end of his road in the village, drove on home and went straight to bed.

The following morning, about half past eight, there was a telephone call which my wife took. It was John's wife – the John I had given a lift to. She was in a terrible state and asked if my wife could go over and stay with her for a few hours. She had just heard that her husband had been killed in a multiple car crash near Winchester at about 6.30 the evening before.

I'd picked John up on the road two and a half hours after that.

TUTOR:	Now listen again and check your answers. Ready? (*Anecdote repeated on tape.*)
TUTOR:	Questions 6–15. Look at the statements and questions and listen to a technology correspondent being interviewed on a radio features programme. But first, read the statements and questions carefully.★
	Now listen to the interview and complete the statements or answer the questions as briefly as you can. In most cases you can use figures or just one or two words. Ready?
INTER.:	Good evening, and welcome again to 'Industry Today'. And in this, the fourth in the series, we're going to look at something which many think, and some fear, will be the picture of a great deal of our industry in the future: The One-Man Factory. With me in the studio I have Barry King the technology correspondent for one of our national weekly newspapers. Barry, welcome to the programme.
BARRY:	Thank you for inviting me.
INTER.:	Now I gather that Britain's first fully-automated factory, in which robots and computers do virtually everything, was opened in Colchester in 1982. Can you tell us something about that?
BARRY:	Yes, that's quite right. It was the first factory in Britain to introduce a flexible manufacturing system. FMS for short. That's the latest jargon for the fully-automated factory you mentioned. The important thing is that most of the work is done by robots, with just a few white-collar operators to, you know, switch things on and check everything's running smoothly.
INTER.:	And how efficient *is* the factory?
BARRY:	Well, the factory makes various engine parts, and it means that a finished component can be produced in three days and with only three men running the production line . . .
INTER.:	Whereas before, it took how long?
BARRY:	Um, before, it took three months to produce finished components, with thirty men. So you can see there is a vast improvement in productivity.

INTER.:	I presume this is not the first factory of its kind in the world.
BARRY:	No. Not surprisingly, the most famous system is the Fanuc plant in Japan, where robots controlled by computers make other robots.
INTER.:	That really does sound like science fiction.
BARRY:	Yes, it does. The plant actually makes 100 robots a month with the very minimum intervention by humans. During the night shift, for example, just one man does in effect the jobs of 200.
INTER.:	That's quite staggering, but also alarming, I think, because it must make one look at the increasing problems of unemployment, which I want to return to in this programme. But for the moment, what about cost? How expensive is it to set up a factory of this kind?
BARRY:	It's fantastically expensive, but the British government is helping out. The Colchester factory, for example, received a government grant of £3 million. But I should add that, not only will it produce its own goods, but it will also act as a showpiece for other companies interested in FMS . . .
INTER.:	A flexible manufacturing system.
BARRY:	Yes. So they'll be able to go and inspect it. I must say here that the Department of Industry has set aside something like £60 million towards development and capital costs, and a large number of firms are applying for grants already.
INTER.:	Well, that sounds very promising. But what about other firms? Are there any other examples you can give us?
BARRY:	Yes. Rolls-Royce has opened an automated plant at Derby which is doing very well. They've already improved their productivity by 28 per cent, with which they're naturally very pleased.
INTER.:	Yes, that really is the kind of figure no doubt most manufacturers would . . .
TUTOR:	Now listen again and check your answers. Ready? (*Interview repeated on tape.*)
TUTOR:	Questions 16–18. Read the three multiple-choice items and then listen to a radio news item. But first read the items.★
	Now listen and answer the multiple-choice items. Ready?
NEWSREADER:	Traffic was brought to a halt today for four hours in the old market town of Oakton. Demonstrators protesting at years of delays in providing the town with a by-pass packed roads in the centre of the town, preventing traffic from flowing in or out. Such was the volume of protesters – it was estimated there were something like 7,000 at one time – that police were powerless to do anything. Only when the protest rally broke up late this afternoon was traffic again allowed to flow through the town. A report now from our reporter in Oakton, John Jones.
JOHN JONES:	The townspeople of Oakton have had enough. That was the clear message of the protest rally today which attracted more than 7,000 participants – not only townspeople, but also many from outlying villages. Oakton is on the most direct route between two of our main ports and therefore increasingly used by heavy lorries, juggernauts and holiday-makers. It's also one of the oldest market towns in this part of the country, and as such, the centre is made up of houses and other buildings, many of which were built in the Middle Ages. Ten years ago the town was promised a by-pass, but successive governments and reports have held up proceedings and now, ten years later, there is still no sign of the by-pass. I spoke to Ray Griffiths, one of the town councillors.
RAY GRIFFITHS:	What amazes me is the fact that we've been promised a new by-pass on so many occasions, and still nothing's happened. It's very depressing. We can see our old town beginning to

suffer badly from the traffic that ploughs through here every day. But it's pure exasperation that's led us today to protest in the way we have done. *And*, by the way, it's the Council that's led the protest this time. All of us! Against the Government!

JOHN JONES: So the people of Oakton have made their feelings felt. It's now up to the Government. John Jones. Oakton.

TUTOR: Now listen again and check your answers. Ready?
(*News item repeated on tape.*)

TUTOR: And that's the end of Unit 9 Test.

Answers

Part 1: 1 D; 2 A; 3 B; 4 C; 5 D

Part 2: 6 robots and computers; 7 3 days; 8 3; 9 3 months; 10 30 men; 11 100 robots; 12 one man; 13 £3 million; 14 about/approximately £60 million; 15 28%

Part 3: 16 D; 17 B; 18 C

Suggested marking scheme

Part 1: Score 2 marks for each correct answer to give a possible maximum score of 10 marks.

Part 2: Score 1 mark for each correct answer to give a possible maximum of 10 marks.

Part 3: Score 2 marks for each correct answer to give a possible maximum of 6 marks.

Possible total maximum for the whole test: 26 marks.

UNIT 10 Mind over Matter

PAPER 5: **INTERVIEW**

Aims of the Unit
1 To give further practice in discussing photos and further familiarise students with three kinds of possible questions on the photo.
2 To continue opportunities for discussion work and role plays of the kind that may form the third part of the Interview Paper.
3 To look at word stress in related nouns and verbs.
4 To give further practice in dealing with passages.
5 Grammar: to review some variations on standard *if*-clauses.
6 To expand students' knowledge of vocabulary connected to the topic of *Mind over Matter*.

Coursebook pp 68–69

Exercise 1 This discussion is intended as a warm-up exercise to get students thinking about the topic of the Unit. As such, it doesn't need to last more than 5–10 minutes.

Exercise 2 **Classroom treatment**
1 Revise the expressions for asking for repetition, expressing assumptions, etc. (Unit 5) before doing the pair work.
2 Students could do this pair work with one taking the role of the examiner and the other that of examinee.

Exercise 3 **Classroom treatment** Students could have different partners from Exercise **2** for this activity. Remember to give them time to write down questions about photo B.

Coursebook pp 70–71

Exercise 1 In the third part of the Interview students could be asked to read a short text such as this one and then take part in a discussion on its contents.

Style of text: direct, informative

Register: neutral

Focus vocabulary
to bask: to sit or lie in enjoyable heat or light
to broil: to (cause to) be very hot or too hot
recurring: that returns or crops up again and again

to nudge: to touch or push gently especially with one's elbow, especially in order to call a person's attention or give a signal

untapped: not used or drawn from

a breed: a kind or class of animal (or plant) usually developed under the influence of man

Classroom treatment Prior to the discussion students could be asked to do as suggested in the passage i.e.

1 close their eyes and repeat . . .;
2 close their eyes and imagine how they themselves would feel if there were no medicines;
3 list suggestions.

Exercise 2
Jigsaw reading This activity provides further training in oral summary work, reporting and practice for the third part of the Interview Paper. Encourage students to look up in a dictionary words which are essential to their comprehension of their extracts, but only after they have tried to work out their meaning from the context. (See page 30 of TG for an explanation of Jigsaw reading.)

Style of text: factual, descriptive, anecdotal

Register: neutral, slightly medical

Focus vocabulary

Extract a)

to master: to gain as a skill

migraine: a severe and repeated headache, usually with pain only on one side of the head or face, and typically with disorder of the eyesight

homely: simple, not grand

to feed back: to provide information about the result of a set of actions, passed back to the person (or machine) in charge, so that changes can be made if necessary

become attuned to: become used to or ready for

a splinter: a small needle-like piece broken off something

Extract b)

a device: an instrument, especially one that is cleverly thought out

feedback: see above

a layer: a thickness of some material laid over a surface

a faith healer: a person who treats disease by prayer or religious faith

to detect: to find out, to notice

Extract c)

to heal: to (cause to) become healthy

innate: which someone was born with

to graze: to break the surface of (especially the skin) by rubbing against something, by accident or on purpose

to bump: to strike or knock with force or violence

to dispense: to deal out, give out

Extract d)

a jaw: one of the two bony parts of the face in which the teeth are set

cancer: a diseased growth in the body

to back up: to support

to overtake: to reach suddenly and unexpectedly

potent: strongly effective

Classroom treatment

1 Divide students into groups of four.
2 Make sure each student knows which extract he/she should read.

3 Students take notes of main points.

4 Students report their extracts to one another working from their notes or memory only and explaining any new vocabulary in English.

Exercise 3   **Classroom treatment** You could allow students a few minutes to think about the statement or even to jot down their ideas about it before beginning the discussion. The discussion could be done with the class as a whole or else initially in pairs prior to a whole group discussion.

Coursebook pp 72–73

Grammar   These kinds of *if*-clauses occur quite regularly in Section A of the Use of English Paper.

Exercise 1   **Classroom treatment** Students could be asked to study this exercise at home or it could be read through with them in class.

Exercise 2   **Classroom treatment** This exercise could be done orally first with the whole class and then students could write the sentences, or students could write the sentences first and then the class as a whole could check what they have written.

Answers

1 Supposing you could heal people like that, what would you do?
2 Had I not seen it with my own eyes, I would never have believed it.
3 But for the faith healer, she would never have lived.
4 Believe in it, or/otherwise you'll never be able to do it.
5 Should you want to know more, I can tell you who to write to.
6 If only I could believe in mind over matter.
7 Suppose you had seen the fakir pour water round the tent, what would you have thought?
8 Should you require any further information, please telephone us.
9 As long as you promise not to laugh, I'll show you the photos.
10 Providing you think positively, you can do it.

Vocabulary Exercise 1   The first set of nouns and verbs, which differ in their stress pattern only, follow the pattern of the noun being stressed on the first syllable and the verb on the second syllable. Point out to students the effects English word stress has on pronunciation. In lexical words (such as nouns, verbs, adjectives, adverbs) one syllable only carries the main stress and the other words (prepositions, articles, pronouns, auxiliary verbs, etc.) have a weaker stress or none at all.

N.B. The sentences in the box on page 73 of the Coursebook are not good style primarily because of the repetition of the same word. In a sentence such as *They won't permit you to do that without a permit*, the verb *permit* might be replaced by the verb *allow*, or the noun *a permit* by *a licence*. The second set of nouns and verbs given differ not in stress but in form, spelling and pronunciation.

Classroom treatment

1 Some discussion of English pronunciation along the lines indicated above may be useful.
2 You could do some choral repetition practice on the different noun–verb pairs before beginning the task as indicated in the Coursebook.

Exercise 2
Game: Read that!

Object of the game Students must read aloud, with correct stress and pronunciation, sentences written by other students.

Conduct of the game

1 Divide the class into groups of 3 or 4.
2 Each group writes on a piece of paper e.g. 6 sentences, each containing 3 or 4 of the nouns and verbs given on page 73. The sentences should not be too long, but they should make sense, however loosely.
3 The groups exchange their pieces of paper and try to read aloud the sentences written on the piece of paper they receive.

N.B. This game could also be played between pairs.

Exercise 3

In the second part of the Interview Paper students will no longer have to read an extract aloud but they will be given a mark on their pronunciation, stress and intonation in the interview as a whole, so pronunciation practice is still relevant. They will be given an extract to read silently and asked to 'situate' it, i.e. tell the examiner what kind of publication or speech situation it probably comes from, who might have written or said it and to whom.

Classroom treatment

1 Explain to students what is involved in 'situating' the extract.
2 Students read the extract silently to 'situate' it.
3 Students report back on extract's situation and gist.

Possible answer This extract is definitely written English. The elaborate sentence construction shows this. It is also formal. It probably comes from a leader article in a serious newspaper e.g. *The Times* or a serious magazine. It is too unscientific in its language to come from a scientific publication.

Coursebook pp 74–75

Exercise 1

Classroom treatment Students could work on the photo initially in pairs. One student could cover the questions and just look at the photo while the other looks at the questions and the photo, and asks the questions as if he/she were the examiner. After approximately half the questions have been asked, the students could then change roles. After this pair work the students could answer the questions as a class. This will give each student an idea of the range and fullness of possible answers.

Exercise 2

Suggested Answers

Passage a): Neutral to slightly informal, probably written language, may be an excerpt from a magazine article or a letter to a newspaper or magazine. *Comment and discussion:* opinions on the value of diet; giving further information about diet; personal experiences of the effect of diet.

Passage b): Informal spoken language (use of *this dreadful ringing* = a dreadful ringing, introductory *Anyway . . .* , and *in the end she ended up*), probably an extract from a conversation or discussion. *Comment and discussion:* opinions on the efficacy of faith healers; other possible explanations of the disappearance of the ringing in her ears; recounting any similar experiences.

Passage c): Formal language, probably written, although could be spoken if part of a formal debate or something similar. Probably an excerpt from a letter to a serious newspaper. *Comment and discussion:* opinions on wisdom of government intervention in such matters; describing situation of such practitioners in candidate's own country; personal opinions.

Exercise 3 See page 48 (Unit 5) of this Teacher's Guide.
Game: Just a minute!

Exercise 4 **Classroom treatment**
Role play 1 It may be necessary to explain to students what playing a role involves (i.e. taking on the part of someone else) and that it is a possible activity in the third part of the Interview Paper.
2 Make sure students make brief but adequate notes. Role plays will backfire if they are not sufficiently well prepared.
3 Review the language needed for presenting an argument, questioning and interrupting. (See also Coursebook pages 15 and 30.)
4 Students conduct the role play in pairs as indicated in the Coursebook.

UNIT 11 Television, Films and Photography

Aims of the Unit 1 To prepare students for questions on author's style, attitude, purpose and intended audience as may occur in Section B of the Reading Comprehension Paper and Section B of the Use of English Paper.

2 To focus students' attention on connotations and their contribution to the message of what someone writes or says.

3 To consolidate the approaches to vocabulary introduced in Units 1 and 6 i.e. guessing the meaning of words through context, vocabulary areas and collocation.

4 To provide students with practical tips and advice on how to tackle the Proficiency Reading Comprehension Paper.

5 To expand students' knowledge of vocabulary connected to the topic of *Television, Films and Photography*.

Coursebook pp 76–77

Style Some of the multiple-choice questions in Section B of the Reading Comprehension Paper may focus not so much on what a passage says but how it says it i.e. style. This is why much of this Unit concentrates on style.

Exercise 1 **Background information** Text A is an extract from the novel *The Four-Gated City* by Doris Lessing. Doris Lessing, born in 1919, has written many novels. Her main theme is a study of life in South Africa and Britain seen from a left-wing, feminist viewpoint. Text B is from Anthony Burgess' book *1985*. Anthony Burgess is a British author, born in 1917, who has also written many novels, the best known of which is probably *A Clockwork Orange*.

Questions 1–6 are concerned with author's attitude, tone, purpose and intended audience as well as with gist reading. Question 7 contains more detailed work on author's style.

Text A

Style of text: persistent, highly rhythmed

Register: neutral

Focus vocabulary

a flicker: an unsteady movement backwards and forwards (of a light or flame)
bland: (of food) not hurting the stomach and without much taste

Text B

Style of text: descriptive, harsh

Register: mostly neutral, but colloquial in parts

Focus vocabulary

to snarl: (of an animal) to make a low angry sound while showing the teeth; (of a person) to speak or say in an angry bad-tempered way *to curse:* to swear; use bad language

'Action': an order given on film sets to start filming

Classroom treatment Do questions 1–6 as indicated in the Coursebook. For question 7, students would probably benefit from working in groups so that they can discuss different interpretations with one another and their reasons for these interpretations.

Answers

Text A

1 The author is opposed to TV as she (Doris Lessing) thinks its constant stream of images deprives reality of meaning.
2 *sameness, nothingness, humanity . . . a meaningless flicker, play, impossible to tell the difference between . . . falsehood, bland, meaningless, steamed white bread,* etc.
3 serious, weary, cynical.
4 lines 11–20 are serious. The whole passage is wearily resigned. Cynicism shows in the reference to a visitor from Mars, in the presentation of life as acting, in the view of the media, and in the references to violence and death.
6 The passage seems like some kind of sociological commentary, possibly in a newspaper or magazine rather than in a book on sociology, since the style of the passage is too novel-like for such a book.
7 1 Through its use of constantly changing short phrases.
  2 To give the impression of manipulated minds that could be treated like the TV i.e. switched on, switched off, etc.
  3 To show that the author considers neither plays nor life to be real on TV.
  4 By talking about changing costumes or settings or actors; as if everything on TV were devised and staged like different scenes in a theatre play.

Text B

1 The author seems to think that TV reporting deprives subjects of their seriousness as they are all considered only from the point of view of whether they will make good pictures and images or not.
2 *act, Really Real when Seen on the Screen, smart red hair, great act . . . for the camera, thumbs up . . . Action,* etc.
3 humorous, ironical, serious.
4 Humour shows in the picture painted of the policemen 'chewing their straps' (of their helmets), in the contrast between Bev's confident appearance and jelly legs, and in the presentation of the strikers and the TV crew as if they were sets of actors on a stage. Irony shows in these phrases: *this act would have no validity . . . screen; a great act of . . . cursing; the sound recordist didn't record . . . stock; Action.* Seriousness is shown in the choice of the subject matter which is a criticism of TV and possibly of the conduct of industrial disputes.
6 The passage seems like an extract from a novel or short story. Its style is too full for it to be a newspaper report and the use of names could indicate some kind of fiction.
7 1 Legs that feel weak and shaky.
  2 They seem like unwilling participants or victims.
  3 This phrase has the connotation of advertising language, even of an advertising jingle.
  4 There could be various connotations: an advert for hair shampoo; casual but fashionable; a potentially angry character.
  5 To give the reader a better idea of the characters of Bev and Fairclough, and of the relationship between them. Also maybe to make fun of the new syllabus.
  6 Again there are various possible connotations; tied up dogs or lions; angry, strong and frustrated. We get the impression that the strikers are somewhat like wild animals. They are shown to the reader in a bad light.
  7 Filming. See above in *Focus vocabulary.*

Exercise 2
Connotations
The *Longman Dictionary of Contemporary English* defines a connotation as follows: a meaning or idea suggested by a word or thing in addition to the formal meaning or nature of the word or thing: *The bad connotations of the word* 'SKINNY' *are quite different from the good connotations of the word* 'SLIM'. Clearly the understanding of connotations therefore forms an important part in understanding the message of a piece of writing. Connotations may influence answers in Sections A and B of the Reading Comprehension Paper and also Section B of the Use of English Paper.

Exercise 3 3 **Suggested answers**
1 news = neutral; propaganda = negative (biased news used to win people over to one's side)
2 a journalist = neutral; a newsmonger = negative (someone who deals in scandal or does anything to get news)
3 to edit = positive (careful work) *and* negative (censure); to write = neutral; to scribble = negative (careless)
4 to stroll = positive (lazy and easy) *and* negative (aimless, slothful); to prowl = negative (suspicious, dishonest); to wander = neutral
5 a scent = positive (nice smell); a stench = negative (awful smell); a smell = neutral
6 a bureaucrat = negative (unhelpful, unfriendly person); a technocrat = positive (efficient) *and* negative (too efficient and machine-like); a civil servant = neutral *and* negative (someone who's lazy and lives off the state)
7 to educate = neutral; to enlighten = positive (to take out of a state of dark ignorance); to indoctrinate = negative (to brainwash)

Coursebook pp 78–79

General discussion
The aim here is to prompt discussion on what could well be a topic for a composition in the Composition Paper or a discussion in the Interview Paper, and to show students the variety of styles that can occur in writing; this passage is much more impartial than those on pages 76 and 77. A final aim is to show students that connotations are not only things which authors work with, but something which we all carry around in our heads and which colour our view of things. To fit in with the aims of the page and the Unit, the tasks set on the passage focus on students' reactions to the passage much more than on detailed reading comprehension. For this reason we recommend you not to do any further work on the passage than that suggested in the Coursebook.

Discussion on a text
Style of text: thoughtful, explanatory

Register: neutral

Focus vocabulary: none

Classroom treatment
1 The General Discussion could be done with the whole class.
2 The discussion on the text could be done in small groups before answers are compared with the class as a whole.

Answers
1 Someone connected with film censoring.
3 See above *Style of text*. The passage makes no use of connotation in keeping with its style, as the author is trying to provide a factual and clear-minded account of his work that does not unfairly colour anybody's opinions.
4 Perhaps from an autobiography or an article in a serious magazine.

Vocabulary This page provides a revision of different approaches to vocabulary studied in Units 1 and 6.

Style of text: narrative, personal

Register: casual, language of photography

Focus vocabulary

a pathfinder: a person who discovers new ways of doing things

cliquey: related to or being like a clique

a posturer: someone who pretends to be something he/she is not

patronage: the support given by a patron

dreary: sad or saddening, dull, uninteresting

to court: to pay attention to (an important or influential person) in order to gain favour, advantage, approval, etc.

not to lift a finger: not to make any effort to help when necessary

vintage: the past time or age to which someone or something belongs

a snapshot: an informal picture taken with a hand-held camera

posterity: descendants, future generations

crooked/'krʊkɪd/: dishonest

fraud: deceitful behaviour for the purpose of gain, which may be punishable by law

Suggested answers

Exercise 2 No, not really. She seems rather cynical about it.

Exercise 3 1 As above in *Focus vocabulary.*

    2 *a pathfinder* = pioneering work, adventurous, courageous, innovative, individual

      cheap = dirty, valueless, common

      a posturer = a hypocrite, dishonest

      paperwork = boring, meticulous, banal but essential work

      tea drinking = a ritual, formality

    3 *photographs, to reproduce, pictures, shots, exposure, a photographer, an engine of creation, depth of field, film, snapshot, view-camera, portrait*

      Words used with double meaning: *exposure, engine of creation, depth of field.* These words are used with double meaning to show how much photography had become part of Maude's life and being, and to show how she seemed to be a marketable product much as her photos were.

    4 *to promote:* goods or products are promoted on a market, and people can be promoted from one job to another

      to court: you court dignitaries or potential lovers

      exposure: photos and scandals receive exposure

      vintage: wine, spirits

      crooked: a nose, criminals, a street

Coursebook pp 80–81

Exam guidance Pages 80–83 provide the first of a series of tips and advice to students on how to deal with each Proficiency Exam Paper. This Unit concentrates on Paper 1, and Units 12, 13, 14 and 15 on Papers 2, 3, 4 and 5 respectively. Each *Exam guidance* section takes students through the different parts of the relevant Paper and shows them answers, reasons for answers and methods of procedure. In other words these sections focus not only on the skills and language required by the exam and tips on how to provide this language and these skills, but also on particular exam techniques and procedures. Students must be completely familiar with the lay-out, formats, testing techniques and answering procedures used by the exam in order to approach it with confidence.

Section A   **Classroom treatment**

1 Explain to students why this section is included in the Coursebook along the lines indicated above.

2 Do the Section A test in class within the time limit suggested on page 80, making sure students do not look at the answers on page 81!

3 Students check answers in pairs *without* looking at page 81.

4 Students give their reasons for answering as they did.

5 Students read over the answers and explanations of answers on page 81, or you read the answers and explanations with them.

6 Read through the 10 Golden Rules for Reading Comprehension Section A on pages 80–81 with the class as a whole.

7 Answer any queries students may have on this part of Paper 1, pointing out to students that Rules 1–7 are purely procedural rules, so that they realise the importance of correct procedure in the exam.

Coursebook pp 82–83

Section B   **Classroom treatment** As for Section A *or* before step 6, see if students can provide the 'Golden Rules' for this Section of the Paper before they read them. In this way students will read the advice given more attentively and be more involved in thinking out exam procedure.

UNIT 12 People, Places, Experiences, Events

PAPER 2: **COMPOSITION**

Aims of the Unit
1 To prepare students to write descriptive and narrative compositions by focusing on detailed and exact vocabulary; careful composition planning, progression and paragraphing; certain stylistic devices; time words in narratives and composition content.
2 To revise the language, style and planning of the composition types introduced in Units 2 and 7.
3 To provide students with practical tips and advice on how to tackle the Proficiency Composition Paper.
4 To expand students' knowledge of vocabulary connected to the topic of *People, Places, Experiences, Events.*

Coursebook pp 84–85

Exercises 1, 2, 3, 4 The purpose of all the activities on page 84 is to get students to reflect on what makes narratives and descriptions interesting. Students often have difficulty in writing these kinds of composition well and this is mainly because their work lacks direction, purpose and detail. Good composition planning and the use of exact vocabulary can do much to overcome this.

Exercise 2 **Suggested answers**
Students might suggest any of the following; detail, purpose, involvement, personal revelations, a story with a difference, vividness of description.

Exercise 3 The difference between a narration and a description is that a narration will contain some kind of sequence of events whereas a description holds, however briefly, to one moment in time. Many pieces of writing are a mixture of description and narration. Whether these particular titles are descriptive or narrative will depend on what the writer decides to put into the composition, but they are likely to be:
1 narrative and descriptive;
2 narrative and descriptive;
3 mainly narrative;
4 mainly descriptive;
5 mainly descriptive;
6 mainly narrative.

Exercise 4 1 Possibly because he was upset at seeing so many young people who seem to have settled in the Bowery.
2 Probably pity or compassion.

Analysing a description This passage is intended to make students aware of the power of style and language, to give them ideas for content and help them to see progression in descriptions.

Style of text: intimate, detailed, personal, poetic in parts

Register: fairly formal

Cultural information

Tennyson: Alfred Lord Tennyson, (1809–92), English poet.

Exercise 1 **Classroom treatment** This exercise would be good for discussion with the class as a whole as this will reveal various interpretations of the passage and opinions about its paragraphing.

Possible answers

Exercise 1 2 Each paragraph has a different focus; the first is mainly a physical description, the second a character description, and the third a description of the influence his mother had on the author.

Exercise 2 Features present in the passage:

1 Use of contrast (contrasting traits of mother's character)
2 A climax (the strong and valuable influence his mother had on him)
3 Variety of sentence length (short sentences for the description of his mother's nervous energy, longer sentences for the description of his mother's influence on him)
4 Precise descriptive vocabulary
5 Personal revelations
8 A conclusion (the last sentence)
9 Quickly moving sentences (see above: variety of sentence length)
10 Images (*a servant girl born to silk, the edge of gold, a jewelled bird, the eyes of orchids, I absorbed the whole earth through her jaunty spirit*)

Features *not* present in the passage:

6 A switch from narrative to dialogue
7 A striking opening sentence

Coursebook pp 86–87

Choosing appropriate vocabulary The purpose of page 86 is as its title indicates: a focus on well-chosen vocabulary. The passage in Exercise **3** will not necessarily contain better vocabulary and phrases than those produced by the students in Exercise **2**; its purpose is to spur comparison, discussion and vocabulary study.

Style of text: dramatic

Register: neutral

Focus vocabulary

to grip: to take a very tight hold of
to loosen from moorings: to release from attachments
to drain out: to (cause to) flow off gradually or completely
a whirl: a very fast movement round and round
to croak: to speak with a rough voice as if one has a sore throat
dumbly: without speaking, stupidly
to leap out: to jump out

Cultural information

Kensington High Street: this is a main shopping street in London
'You feeling ill lady?': (=Are you feeling ill, Madam?) The phrase is meant to reflect real working-class London speech.

Exercise 3   **Classroom treatment**

The comparing could be done initially in pairs and then lead on to a general class discussion on the use of vocabulary in the passage.

Exercise 4   This exercise is best done initially in pairs and then the discussion of answers with the class as a whole.

Exercise 4   **Suggested answers**

1 *gripped, loosened from its moorings, to recede, down a long misty tunnel, the colour seemed to drain out . . . , a whirl of lightheadedness, bloodless daylight, leapt*

2 Each paragraph has a different focus; the first is about what happened when the woman read the news, the second about her leaving the building, and the third about the taxidriver's reaction to her.

3 *For a moment, as soon as, still, when*
   Synonyms: for a moment: for a second/an instant
                as soon as: no sooner

Change in sentence construction: *No sooner did she see her car than . . .*

N.B.	*Phrases given*	*Synonyms*
	immediately	straight away
	finally	eventually, in the end
	gradually	slowly, bit by bit
	while	as
	eventually	finally, in the end
	for a while	for a moment

Note: *Eventually* has been repeated deliberately in this exercise as it is frequently misused by students. While the above words may be synonymous they don't all carry the same degree of formality. This should be pointed out to students.

Structuring a description

Style of text: part note form, part connected prose; detailed; descriptive; factual

Register: neutral

Focus vocabulary

to pour forth: to flow out
a tint: a pale or delicate shade of a colour
mean: poor or poor-looking as of a building
to twinkle: to shine with an unsteady light that rapidly changes from bright to faint; (stars twinkle)
a glimpse: a quick look or an incomplete view of
fiery: flaming and violent

Cultural information

Sheffield: This is a city in the north of England which played an important part in the British Industrial Revolution of the 18th and 19th centuries. Its main industries were steel and iron.

George Orwell: George Orwell is the author of many pieces of writing, the best known of which are *Animal Farm* and *1984*. He spent some time walking around Britain to become better acquainted with its social conditions.

Exercise 1   **Classroom treatment** This exercise is best done initially in pairs.

Possible answers

1 landscape/skyscape, hilliness, foundries, state of small workshops.

2 One possibility for paragraphing is:
   para. 1 from the beginning to *in the town* (line 13);
   para. 2 from line 13 to *like stars* (line 18);

para. 3 from line 18 to *into rails* (line 23);

para. 4 from line 23 to the end.

Another possibility is to combine paragraphs 2 and 3 above.

3   Line 1   Subject needed for *had*.

     Lines 1–2   Contents of brackets need to be incorporated into the text.

     Lines 7–13   This series of short sentences would need combining into longer ones.

     Lines 13–14 Contents of brackets would have to be incorporated into the text.

     Line 16   *etc.* would need fleshing out.

     Line 20   Contents of brackets would need incorporating into the text.

     Line 23   Contents of brackets would need incorporating into the text.

     Line 25   *i.e.* would probably have to be changed. Depending on the choice of style the references to *I* might also be omitted and the same information incorporated into the text in different ways.

The changes mentioned above are the minimum necessary.

4 *appalling, pouring forth, a rosy tint, mean, twinkle, splendid, rosy, a glimpse, fiery serpents of red-hot and white-hot*, etc.

Exercise 2   **Classroom treatment** We suggest you move round the class checking students' written work during steps 2 and 3 and advising where necessary.

Coursebook p 88

Exam guidance   The *Exam guidance* here aims to provide students with tips and advice as to exam procedure: revision of language, planning and composition types; and familiarisation with the exam format. The four composition titles in the Composition Paper on this page are worked on successively and in different ways on pages 89–91.

Classroom treatment As these pages contain important exam advice, it is recommended that they should be handled in class rather than set as homework reading. This is to make sure that all students have the opportunity to read and understand them thoroughly as well as to voice and have explained any doubts they may have. N.B. Do not ask students to write the compositions given in the exam Paper.

Answers

1 2; 2 2 hours; 3a) approximately 5 minutes; b) approx. 10 minutes; c) approx. 35 minutes; d) approx. 10 minutes; e) approx. 10 minutes; f) approx. 35 minutes; g) approx. 10 minutes. 4 No, and with careful planning and checking it isn't necessary; 5c) Students may often be tempted to choose appealing titles without thinking whether they can actually handle them from the linguistic point of view. Encourage them to evaluate titles for both their linguistic and their information content.

N.B. Notice the relatively short amount of time given over to actual composition writing. Students must spend time on careful planning and checking. In this way they will not require more writing time and will produce better quality work. This should be pointed out to students.

Coursebook p 89

A revision of composition writing

Exercise 1   **Answers** There can be no set answer to these exercises since there are several different ways of organising the points.

Exercise 2   **Answers**

5   a) is unacceptable. It clearly intends to depart from the title of the composition, which therefore would be judged irrelevant.

    b) as a)

    c) a classic opener for this kind of composition.

    d) another classic opener.

    e) a personal and relevant introduction

6   *Vocabulary given*

Vocabulary given	Synonyms
firstly	first, first of all, to begin with
in my opinion	to my mind, as far as I'm concerned
in short	in brief
as regards	as for X, as far as X is concerned, regarding X
despite	in spite of
besides	in addition (to)
however	nevertheless
e.g.	for example, for instance
that is to say	in other words, to be precise
lastly	finally, last of all

Coursebook p 90

Exercise 3
Style, planning,
degree of formality,
joining words

Classroom treatment It is best for each student to do all the tasks in this exercise individually before comparing answers with others in the class.

Answers and possible answers

1 This is a sample of the letter students might write. Clearly, students will produce different letters: the important thing to check is that answers are not only grammatically correct and relevant, but that they are also written in the required formal style. (The parts in italics are possible completions.)

Dear *Mr/Mrs/Ms/Miss Smith,*

    (I would like to) thank you (very much) for your letter of 3rd September. First *of all,* I *would* like to say *how* very surprised I was to receive your letter. Our company rarely receives complaints and it was *therefore* most disturbing for us to receive *such* a letter.

    I would like to *deal* with your points one *by* one; *firstly/first of all/first, with regard to/regarding* what you said about the quality of our service, *may* I say that our company has always done its *best/utmost* to ensure its customers' excellent service. However, you may *feel that your experience warrants your complaint about bad service* and this I very much regret.

    Secondly, *our company does everything possible to maintain exceptionally high standards of hygiene. Indeed, regular inspections are carried out to ensure we keep to international standards, and we have even been awarded prizes in this area.*

Thirdly, *as for your remarks regarding our safety precautions, I can only state that the company observes rigidly those laid down by international laws regarding air transport.*

(And) finally/lastly/last of all, as far *as* our prices *are concerned,* I'm afraid we have no control over these as they are fixed by international agreement.

To compensate you for the *inconvenience* you may have experienced, we would be very happy to *offer you a free flight up to the value of £200.* Please *contact me personally with details when and if you decide to take up what we feel is a more than generous offer of compensation.*

We look *forward to hearing from you.*

Yours sincerely,

(Signature)
Public Relations Officer

2 Para. 1: thank and express surprise
   Para. 2: how intend to deal with points raised in letter, defence of company's
            service, regrets as to any exceptional bad service
   Para. 3: defence of company's standards of hygiene mentioning e.g. prizes
            received, obligation to keep to international standards, regular inspection
   Para. 4: defence of company's safety precautions
   Para. 5: defence of company's prices, international agreements
   Para. 6: free flight up to sum of £XXX
            ask to contact with details

3 Formal style:
   I would like . . . how surprised I was . . . such a letter; I would like to deal . . .
   one by one; as regards; may I say; done its utmost; best to ensure; and this I
   very much regret; I'm afraid we . . .; you may have experienced . . .

4 secondly (next, second); thirdly (third); finally (fourthly, lastly, last of all)

5

	Formal letters		*Informal letters*
Begin:	Dear Sir		Dear (first name)
	Madam		Mum/Mother/Dad, etc
	Ms		Uncle/Aunt
	Mrs	+ surname	Grandpa/Grandma
	Miss		
	Mr		

End:	Yours faithfully		(Very) Best wishes,
	Initial(s) + surname + (Mr etc)		Regards,
	(If begun Dear Sir/Madam)		Yours,
			Love,
	Yours sincerely		Lots of love,
	(Title) + initial(s) or		(First name)
	first name + surname		N.B. These informal endings
	(if begun with other forms)		are listed in descending order
			of formality.

Coursebook p 91

Checking your composition This section aims to point out to students the importance of checking their work very carefully. It also aims to build up an awareness of the kind of mistakes they usually make so that they can initially check for these kinds of mistake and eventually even stop making them. There are various categories of mistake; some are typical of all learners of English e.g. those mentioned in Exercise 4, 3; others are typical of learners with a particular mother tongue and are due to mother tongue interference; yet others are peculiar to individual learners. The teacher should help each student realise what mistakes he/she regularly makes. Students need training in the careful checking of their written work as, when checking, they tend to read not what they've written but what they think they've written! They need to try to distance themselves from their work at the checking stage and read it over as if they had never seen it before.

Exercise 4 **Classroom treatment**

1 Discuss the above points with the class as a whole.

2 Steps 1 and 2 should be done individually or in pairs first before answers are checked with the class as a whole.

3 The other steps can be done as indicated in the Coursebook.

Answers

1

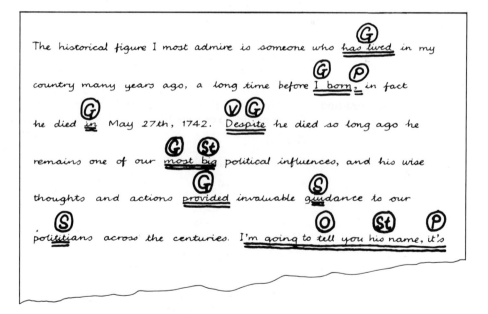

2 The following is one possible version: The historical figure I most admire is someone who lived in my country many years ago, a long time before I was born. In fact, he died on May 27th 1742. Although he died so long ago, he remains one of our major political influences, and his wise thoughts and actions have provided invaluable guidance to our politicians across the centuries. Let me tell you his name: it's . . .

4 One main part is the description of the historical figure. The other main part is explaining why you admire him.

UNIT 13 Preservation and Conservation

Coursebook pp 92–93

Exercise 1 **Classroom treatment** Here are some extra discussion prompts which might be useful for this warm-up exercise:

– Which should be preserved in preference – the Coliseum in Rome or the Roman ruins of a town in Tipaza, Algeria?

– Should the Amazon rain forests be cut down and replaced by cereals, or should they be left as they are?

– Should we preserve whales and seals? Should we conserve oil?, etc.

Exercise 2
Jigsaw reading Besides providing practice in reading for detail and note-taking for summary work, this activity also prepares students for the third part of the Interview Paper through Jigsaw reading. See page 30 of the TG for an explanation of Jigsaw reading.

Text a)

Style of text: factual, discursive

Register: formal

Focus vocabulary

a reservoir: (here) a large supply
to spawn: to produce, especially in large numbers
high-rise (adj.): (of buildings, especially, blocks of flats with several floors) built very high
offspring: a child or children
to breed: to produce young
a stock: a group of animals used for breeding

Text b)

Style of text: factual

Register: technical, formal

Focus vocabulary

sole: having no sharer, being the only one
to saturate: to fill completely so that no more can be held
to crumble: to break into very small pieces, to decay; come to ruin

Text c)

Style of text: factual, discursive

Register: neutral, technical

Focus vocabulary

a trough: a depression
to be tied up with: to be connected with
asbestos: a soft grey material (like a mass of threads) that is dug out of the ground and made into clothes that protect against fire and solid sheets that prevent the spreading of heat

Classroom treatment Each group should contain no more than four people. Instruct students to extract the main points only and not to pay attention to *every* unknown vocabulary item, only those essential for comprehension of the extracts. The meaning of any unknown words should first be worked out from the context and a dictionary consulted only as a last resort. Make sure that students' notes are indeed notes and not long full sentences.

Coursebook pp 94–95

Exercise 1   **Classroom treatment** Join together into larger groups of 12 the three smaller groups who each looked at separate texts in the previous activity. Make sure the reporting is done from notes only and not with reference to the original texts, and also that the students listening take notes of the main points only, as if they were taking notes at a lecture. This is in preparation for the Homework exercise **3**.

Exercise 2   **Classroom treatment** This discussion could be introduced to the students at the same time as Exercise 1. In this way the discussion would follow on naturally from the reporting and the groups of 12 students would be maintained. However, this discussion could also be an interesting class discussion, especially in mixed nationality classes. A further discussion point could be: Can poor countries allow themselves to have a 'Conservation/Preservation Programme'?

Possible answers

Exercise 1   The report should be based on the main points of each extract as follows:

Text a) Zoos can offer unique facilities for amassing information. Certain aspects of animal biology can be studied more easily or only in zoos.
Zoos can provide lots of data if this is well studied and recorded.
Zoos are educationally important.
People raised in cities might only have zoos to remind them that they share this planet.
Zoos can help in conservation, through the breeding of animals in zoos and also by stocking up on endangered species.

Text b) Acropolis is threatened more by industrial civilization than ever before.
Dilapidation now so bad that vast conservation scheme essential immediately; technically and scientifically beyond Greek means, therefore appeal to world for help. Chemical pollution has done more damage in 20 years than anything else ever before.
Caryatids, now protected in plastic and plaster, should go into as yet unbuilt museum.
Cecrops frieze difficult to transfer to museum because crumbling, but of great value to Greece because symbol.

Text c) Air pollution less serious than 100 years ago, but may get worse because of combustion in cars, modern man's legs.
Also endangered by industrial and agricultural air pollution.
Chief causes remain car and generation of electricity. Electricity generation based largely on fossil fuels and likely to treble by 1990, still based on fossil fuels.

Use of English:
Blank-filling
Exercises 1 and 2

This type of exercise occurs regularly in Section A of the Proficiency Use of English Paper. While it is essentially a test of grammar, to get answers right students need to read the whole sentences carefully so as to pick up clues for the answer from all possible sources. Students tend not to read beyond the blank and for this reason they must be encouraged to read the whole sentence.

Classroom treatment

1 Read through with the students the advice given in the Coursebook to make sure they see the relevance of all the points made and to give them the opportunity to voice any doubts they may have.
2 Each student should write the answers to these exercises before they are checked with the class as a whole, so as to give everyone the opportunity to follow the necessary thinking process. N.B. The structures tested in these exercises are all points studied in previous Units of the Coursebook.

Possible answers

Exercise 1
1 pleased/surprised/delighted I was
2 of being; of the fact that he was
3 though she was; as she was
4 to be seen/found
5 having been/gone to
6 The sooner
7 it not been for; there not been; we not got caught in
8 angry/frustrated/exasperated was he/did he feel
9 did I know/realise
10 they wouldn't have had to; they wouldn't have been forced/obliged to

Exercise 2
1 better go; be (well) advised to go
2 have been doing/going/driving
3 Congratulations on getting/passing
4 be grateful/pleased if you
5 there must have been; there was; there might have been

Coursebook pp 96–97

Exam guidance
Section A

The four exercises included in the test, although shorter, follow the same style and order as the exercises in Section A of the Proficiency Use of English Paper.

Classroom treatment

1 Ask students to cover page 97.
2 Students do the four exercises in Section A in the recommended time.
3 Students check their answers with one another and give reasons for their answers.
4 Students look at the answers and explanations of answers on page 97.
5 Discussion of any doubts or queries.

Coursebook pp 98–99

Section B   The style of questions and the order in which they are presented are typical of Section B of the Proficiency Use of English Paper. The *Exam advice* given on page 99 contains important points that students must adhere to. Students must realise the importance of reading comprehension in Section A of the Use of English Paper and also realise the importance throughout the Paper of following the instructions given exactly. You will note that in the advice given for Section B students are recommended to do the summary *before* answering the comprehension questions. This is because we feel that it is important for students to be thinking in terms of general meaning when writing a summary. If students answer comprehension questions on detail before doing the summary it may make it more difficult for them to distinguish main points from detail, whereas if they go straight to the summary they can fall back on their initial general comprehension to provide them with main points.

Classroom treatment As above for Section A.

Exam advice: General   **Classroom treatment** As for *Exam advice* in Units 11 and 12.

UNIT 14 Leisure and Health

Aims of the Unit
1 To give students practice in listening for mood, attitudes and feelings in preparation for the Listening Comprehension Paper.
2 To extend students' acquaintance with formal and informal spoken language in preparation for the Listening Comprehension Paper.
3 To introduce students to the concept of registers of language in preparation for the Listening Comprehension Paper.
4 To provide students with practical tips and advice on how to tackle the Proficiency Listening Comprehension Paper.
5 To expand students' knowledge of vocabulary connected to the topic of *Leisure and Health*.

Coursebook p 100

Exercise 1   The aim of this exercise is to lead into the topic of Leisure and Health and also to familiarise students with working with a chart or grid.

Exercises 1 and 2   **Classroom treatment** These exercises could be done in either of the following ways:
1 Students find out about one another's pastimes by asking one another questions in pairs as indicated in the Coursebook. Results could then be compiled on a chart on the blackboard.
2 Students could all move round the class at the same time each interviewing at least five people, and then these findings could be pooled in general class report backs.

Exercise 3   **Style of text:** conversational

Register: neutral

🖭 Tapescript

TUTOR:	Unit 14. Leisure and Health. Look at page 100, Exercise 3. Look at the questionnaire and listen. You'll hear a man and woman being interviewed in the street. As you listen to their answers, fill in the questionnaire with 'M' for the man's answers, 'W' for the woman's answers. Ready?
INTERVIEWER:	Excuse me.
MAN:	Yes.
INTER.:	I wonder if you and your wife would answer a questionnaire for an opinion poll that we're doing on pastimes and leisure.
MAN:	Yes, of course.
WOMAN:	Well, I don't know, George. It's getting very late, and, you know . . .
INTER.:	Well, if you'd rather not . . .
MAN:	No, no, it's fine. You go ahead.

INTER.:	Well, then, do you agree or disagree with this statement? 'I don't have enough leisure time.'
MAN:	Oh, disagree, definitely. I have plenty of leisure time.
WOMAN:	Well, I don't. I never seem to have time for anything I want to do . . .
MAN:	Yes, dear. Let's get on with it, can we?
INTER.:	Now, can you tell me how often you do the following things: Every day? Once or twice a week? Once a month? Very rarely? Or never? How often do you read a book?
MAN:	Every day.
WOMAN:	How often do I ever have time to read a book? Once in a blue moon, if I'm lucky.
INTER.:	Er, yes. How often do you watch television or listen to the radio?
WOMAN:	Oh, we watch television every evening, don't we, George? We love it!
MAN:	It's all right, if you like everything they put on. But radio. Now that's different. I still think it's great and I listen to it every day in the car.
WOMAN:	I think I only ever turn the radio on once or twice a week.
INTER.:	How about indoor games? Do you ever play cards, or Monopoly, or Scrabble . . . ?
WOMAN:	Oh, very rarely.
MAN:	But I play cards once a month, down at the club.
INTER.:	Video games?
WOMAN:	No, never. We haven't got a video, have we, George?
MAN:	No. But I'd like to buy one. I think they're excellent!
INTER.:	Do either of you play outdoor games? You know, tennis? Golf?
WOMAN:	No, nothing like that, never.
INTER.:	And you, sir?
MAN:	No, I don't play tennis, or anything. But I try to go swimming once a week, and we both go for a long walk about once a month, I suppose.
WOMAN:	Good heavens! I never thought I'd hear him say it! George! – we go for a long walk just occasionally. Certainly not once a month!
MAN:	Yes, she's right, of course. About the walking I mean. But I *do* go swimming once a week.
INTER.:	Now, how often do you do these things? Go to . . .
MAN:	Ouch! I think I've just been stung on my neck!
WOMAN:	Oh, no! Let me have a look.
MAN:	Pheew!
WOMAN:	Yes, there is a sting there. I can see it. A wasp's sting, I think. Just hold on and I'll try and get it out. It won't hurt. Ah, there it is!
MAN:	Phew! I thought you said it wouldn't hurt!
WOMAN:	Well . . . I think we'd better get to the nearest chemist and get something for that. Will you excuse us?
INTER.:	Well, could we quickly finish the questions perhaps?
MAN:	Yes, all right, but very quickly.
INTER.:	Well, as I was saying, how often do you do these things? Go to the cinema?
MAN:	Never.
INTER.:	Go to the theatre, opera or ballet?
MAN:	Ballet? Yuk! No, never.
WOMAN:	No, never. Any of them.
INTER.:	Go to a concert?
WOMAN:	Occasionally.
INTER.:	Go to an art gallery, museum, etc?
MAN:	Oh, about once a month. I enjoy going to museums. Pheew! This is hurting! How many more questions?
INTER.:	Not many. Now, do either of you play an instrument?
WOMAN:	No.

INTER.:	Uh-huh. Do either of you sing in a choir?	
MAN:	No.	
INTER.:	Do you ever go to the beach or a lake?	
WOMAN:	Well, once a year really. We always have a seaside holiday.	
INTER.:	Fine. How about going fishing or hunting?	
WOMAN:	No.	
MAN:	Oh, I love fishing. I can think of nothing better than sitting on a river bank in the pouring rain . . .	
WOMAN:	George! Don't take any notice of him.	
INTER.:	No. Do you go cycling, climbing or anything?	
MAN:	No.	
INTER.:	Do either of you paint?	
MAN:	No. And how many more questions?	
INTER.:	Only one or two. Do you attend a club of any kind?	
MAN:	Yes, a social club twice a week.	
WOMAN:	I go to an antiques club once a month.	
INTER.:	And the last question . . .	
MAN:	About time, too!	
INTER.:	Do you help other people? You know, the elderly, the disabled . . . ?	
WOMAN:	Well, neither of us does at the moment, but I've just put my name down to help at an Old People's Club . . .	
MAN:	I didn't know anything about that! You might have *told* me! Anyway, let's get to that chemist's and get something . . .	
INTER.:	Er, thank you very much!	
TUTOR:	To listen to the interview again, rewind the tape.	

Answers

	MAN	WOMAN
Read a book	Every day	Very rarely
Watch TV	Every day	Every day
Listen to radio	Every day	Once or twice a week
Play indoor games	Once a month	Very rarely
Play video games	Never	Never
Play outdoor games	Never	Never
Go swimming, etc.	Once or twice a week (swimming) Very rarely (walks)	Very rarely
Go to – the cinema,	Never	Never
theatre, etc.	Never	Never
a concert,		Occasionally
an art		
gallery,		
etc.	Once a month	
Play an instrument	Never	Never
Play in an orchestra, etc.	Never	Never
Sing	Never	Never
Go to the beach, etc.	Very rarely	Very rarely
Go fishing, etc.	Never	Never
Go cycling, etc.	Never	
Paint	Never	Never
Attend a club	Once or twice a week	Once a month
Help other people	Never	Never

Coursebook p 101

Listening for mood, attitudes and feelings

In the Listening Comprehension Paper, students may be asked to identify speakers' moods, attitudes or feelings. To be able to do this they will have to understand not only *what* is said but *how* it is said (i.e. intonation), and in some cases to understand intonation that gives a different meaning to the words, as, for example, the man on the tape above when he talks about fishing. It is extremely difficult to give hard and fast rules about what moods and meanings are accompanied by which intonation patterns, as slight differences in speech situations or attitudes can involve slight nuances of meaning and therefore slight changes in the intonation pattern. The Cambridge Examinations Syndicate does not intend to require students to identify unusual or fine distinctions in the meanings of intonation patterns, and with practice and familiarity students quickly come to be able to recognise general intonation patterns accurately.

Exercise 1

Classroom treatment Students should do this task individually first, then compare their answers in pairs then with the group as a whole. It would be helpful if the teacher paused the tape between each different set of sentences, and, if students appear to be having difficulties, to replay the tape immediately after that set of sentences that caused the problems. After students have completed the exercise they could listen to the sentences again and try to repeat them with the correct intonation.

Tapescript

TUTOR:	Look at page 101, Exercise 1.
	Look at the sentences in the boxes and listen carefully. As you listen, write down the mood or feeling you think is being expressed against the numbers you've written down, 1–8.
	Ready?
	One.
SPEAKER:	Well, well!
(*surprised*)	Good heavens!
	Pheew!
	Honestly?
	Did you really?
TUTOR:	Two.
SPEAKER:	Oh, I think it's wonderful!
(*enthusiastic*)	Tennis is a great sport!
	I can't think of anything better!
TUTOR:	Three.
SPEAKER:	Ouch! I've just cut my finger!
(*in pain*)	Phew! I thought you said that wouldn't hurt!
TUTOR:	Four.
SPEAKER:	Ugh! How can you eat that stuff?
(*disgusted*)	Yuk! How can you eat that stuff?
	Eeugh! That looks awful!
TUTOR:	Five.
SPEAKER:	Well, I don't know . . .
(*apprehensive*)	Oh, dear!
TUTOR:	Six.
SPEAKER:	Mm, it's all right, I suppose, if you like that sort of thing.
(*bored*)	Well, I don't worry either way, really.
TUTOR:	Seven.
SPEAKER:	You might have *told* me!
(*annoyed,*	I don't think that's funny at all!
angry)	Would you please close the window!
	He must have know, surely!
TUTOR:	Eight.

SPEAKER:	Oh, yeah! Fantastic!
(*ironic*)	Opera? Oh, I *love* opera. I can't get enough of it.
TUTOR:	Now check your answers with the rest of the class. If you need to listen again, rewind the tape.

Answers

1 surprise; 2 enthusiasm; 3 pain; 4 disgust; 5 apprehension/worry; 6 boredom;
7 anger/annoyance/disapproval; 8 irony/sarcasm

Tapescript

Exercise 2

TUTOR:	Look at page 101, Exercise 2. Listen to these brief extracts from the interview with the man and woman again and answer the four multiple-choice questions. Ready? One.
WOMAN:	Oh, we watch television every evening, don't we, George? We love it!
MAN:	It's all right if you like everything they put on. But radio. Now that's different. I still think it's great and I listen to it every day in the car.
TUTOR:	Two.
WOMAN:	Oh, no! Let me have a look.
MAN:	Pheew!
WOMAN:	Yes, there is a sting there. I can see it.
TUTOR:	Three.
INTER.:	Fine. How about going fishing or hunting?
WOMAN:	No.
MAN:	Oh, I love fishing. I can think of nothing better than sitting on a river bank in the pouring rain . . .
WOMAN:	George!
TUTOR:	Four.
INTER.:	Do either of you paint?
MAN:	No. And how many more questions?
INTER.:	Only one or two.
TUTOR:	Now rewind the tape, listen again and check your answers.

Answers
1 C; 2 B; 3 D; 4 B

Coursebook p 102

Register: formal and informal

Register is a term which is used in linguistics to refer to two different language phenomena. It can be used firstly to refer to the degree of formality of language, and secondly to refer to that language which is distinctive of a particular use. For example, many vocabulary items are peculiar to scientific English. Scientific English also has a particular style and makes a high use of the passive voice. Advertising language on the other hand makes great use of imperatives and superlatives. On these two pages of the Coursebook students will meet both uses of the term *register* as they need to both recognise and produce different levels of formality in spoken language and to be able to associate particular linguistic terms with particular speakers and settings.

Exercise 1   **Style of text:** direct, brisk

Register: neutral

N.B. The use of capitals 'IN MY dieting days . . .': this is a print convention often used in newspapers and magazines to catch the reader's eye.

Suggested answer Because it speeds up your metabolic rate, which means you burn more calories.

Exercise 2   **Classroom treatment** Students could revise what they already know about degrees of formality in language before doing this exercise. They could do this either by referring back to Unit 7, or by trying to summarise and recall as a class the features of formal and informal English, and the teacher could write this summary on the blackboard along the lines the students suggest.

🔘 Tapescript

TUTOR: Look at page 102, Exercise **2**. You're going to hear two people telling someone else about the article in Exercise **1**. Listen to each and say which is using formal and which informal speech. You must give reasons. Ready?
One.

MAN: The article by Geoffrey Cannon about exercise I found most illuminating. What was interesting, I think, was not only that he had taken up running as a result of basically being unable to lose weight by dieting, but that he started to investigate the weight loss which seemed to surprise him. As he said, in theory, exercise is not a particularly effective way of losing weight, and yet in practice it most certainly would seem to be extremely effective. The reason, according to him, is that running, together with certain other types of exercise, increases the metabolic rate and you thus burn more calories.

TUTOR: Two.

WOMAN: I read an article the other day that was very interesting. It was by a man who'd dieted for years, but never lost any weight. But then he took up jogging to keep his weight down. And it worked. He found out that as long as he went running regularly, he could eat and drink what he wanted. Then he began to look into why exercise helps you lose weight. Apparently all the dieting experts say it doesn't work. Well, apparently the reason is that your metabolism speeds up when you run, and that's good for you because it burns up more calories.

TUTOR: Now rewind the tape, listen to them again a little more carefully and pick out some of the features which make one more formal than the other.

Answers and suggested answers The man speaks formally and the woman informally. The man is probably some kind of public figure talking to an audience, whereas we have no information about the woman except that the informality of the way she talks suggests she is probably chatting to a friend.

Exercise 3   **Classroom treatment** You will need to pause the tape to allow students the time to write their answers down.

Possible answers

Formal:

– full grammatical forms: these are used throughout.
– noun constructions: *weight loss*; *the metabolic rate*
– formal vocabulary: *illuminating*; *in theory*; *effective*; *in practice*; *thus*
– more complex language: the length of the sentences and their construction
– conjunctions: *thus*

Informal:

– shortened forms: *doesn't; that's*
– simple verb constructions: *why exercise helps you lose weight; the metabolism speeds up*
– phrasal verbs: *took up; found out; speeds up; burns up; look into*
– informal vocabulary: *that's good for you*
– general vocabulary: *worked; good*
– simple sentences: these are used throughout
– simple conjunctions: *but; then; because*

Coursebook p 103

Register:
'professional varieties'
Exercise 1   **Possible answers**

1 Some women are taking part in some kind of gymnastics class. Because they're all dressed for sport and are in some kind of gym.
2 That the woman in the foreground is the instructor of the class, and that the women are there to lose weight. Pounds means money (£) to Cindy and weight (lbs) to the people in the class.

Exercise 2   **Style of text:** This varies with the different speakers.

Register: This too varies from one speaker to the next.

🔲 Tapescript

TUTOR:	Look at page 103, Exercise 2. You're going to hear people from different professions talking about the boom in the 'Keep-Fit' industry. As you listen, put the number of the speaker against the profession. Ready? One.
LAWYER:	I suspect that it's already fairly common practice for people going along to aerobics and keep-fit classes and suchlike to sign something saying that the organisers will not be liable for damage for permanent injury, etc. But whether such documents are legally binding on either party has yet to be seen. There is already one case going through the courts now of a middle-aged man who enrolled in such a course and suffered a heart attack during the first session. He didn't die, but has been ill since, and he and his wife are claiming against the school . . .
TUTOR:	Two.
SOCIOLOGIST:	What I find so interesting is this sudden surge in the past few years for people um people of all ages, from . . . well, I mean, after school-leaving age . . . from 20 to 80 to keep fit. More and more people are going jogging, swimming regularly, taking up tennis, and so on. And um nowhere is this more noticeable than in the numbers of mainly women going to keep-fit or aerobics classes. Cindy Gilbert's classes, for example, grew from one small class of twelve to a staggering 7,000 participants in 70-odd halls in and around London. This is a clear example of a major change in society itself, and is worthy of study to try to answer questions like: *Is* society coming to terms with increased leisure time? Or is this perhaps only a strange temporary trend?
TUTOR:	Three.

BUSINESSMAN:	One in two of our leading products were certainly in decline, and we were in danger of having to cut back our staff, until there was this new wave of interest in sport and keep-fit. The special gear, kit and clothes we now produce for this market has meant that we have actually increased production and have taken on more staff than we had before. At the moment there is a boom in equipment for the keep-fit movement, and we can hardly keep up with demand. We just hope it continues . . .
TUTOR:	Four.
A DOCTOR:	I am not myself an advocate of dieting. What I recommend to patients often is a change in their way of life, so that they try to get more exercise and balance that with a good varied diet – plenty of vegetables, roughage, fruit and so on. Cut right down on alcohol and try to stop smoking, if they smoke. Of course, some then come back to me with pulled muscles, sprained ankles and the like, but er these are simple things to deal with . . .
TUTOR:	Five.
ARTS COUNSELLOR:	While we're talking about a renewed interest in keep-fit and aerobics, we mustn't forget too there's also been a rise in the number of young people taking up gymnastics quite seriously. And this must soon begin to be reflected in a renewed interest in ballet. At least, I hope it will. Obviously, my own concern is with ballet, opera and music, but keep-fit, aerobics, gymnastics and ballet all have something in common.
TUTOR:	Six.
TOWN PLANNER:	Not so many years ago, a person in my position would have been more concerned with roads, parks, the development of housing estates and so on, but we are now having to think a great deal more about amenities – the provision of sports complexes, landscaping, and so on. My predecessors made some terrible mistakes, which I hope we have learned from now . . .
TUTOR:	Page 103, Exercise 3. Now rewind the tape, listen again and note down words and expressions which the speakers use in connection with their professions.

Answers

1 lawyer; 2 sociologist; 3 businessman; 4 doctor; 5 arts counsellor; 6 town planner.

Exercise 3 Classroom treatment

1 There are many words and expressions in this extract related to each profession. Do not expect or ask students to note each one down. This is not a dictation. Just ask them to note down some typical words so that they can consolidate their understanding of register.

2 Pause the tape after each 'expert' has spoken to give the students time to make their notes.

3 Students could compare their answers in pairs then groups.

Role play Students may have to take part in a role play in the third part of the Interview Paper.

Classroom treatment

1 Divide students into groups of 4 and allot each of them one of the following roles:
  a) the representative of a sports team that hasn't any good facilities at present;
  b) a businessman who already owns the only Leisure Complex in town;
  c) a businessman who wishes to build a cinema on this same site;
  d) the businessman who wishes to build the Leisure Complex.

2 Discuss with the class as a whole the facilities already available in their town, and who would benefit from such a club, and what inconveniences, if any, it could bring. You may even want to propose an exact site where the Leisure Complex would be built.

3 Explain to students who the four participants in each group are.

4 Students prepare their arguments individually or in groups of particular businessmen, sports team representatives, etc.

5 Revise the language of agreeing, disagreeing, giving opinions, interrupting, etc.

6 Put students into groups each containing the four different roles.

7 The role play takes place.

8 Report back – each group tells the class the conclusions they have reached.

Coursebook pp 104–105

Exam guidance   **Classroom treatment**

1 Students cover the answers and explanations of answers for Part 1.

2 Students do Part 1 of the test.

3 Students compare and discuss their answers.

4 Students read the answers and Explanations of answers.

5 Follow the same procedure for Part 2 of the test.

🎞 Tapescript

TUTOR:

Unit 14. Exam guidance.
Look at page 104. Questions 1–10. You're going to hear part of a talk and will have to tick whether the statements are true or false. But first, read through the ten True/False statements.*
Now listen to the talk and tick whether the statements are true or false, according to what you hear. Ready?

WOMAN VIOLIN
TEACHER:

Ladies and gentlemen, and particularly children: welcome. I'm thrilled to see so many of you here this afternoon, and sincerely hope that, when I've told you about the classes and the method, many of you children will want to begin as soon as you can.

As you are aware, we at this school teach the violin through the system made famous by Dr Suzuki. It's a system based on a belief that there is no such thing as inborn talent, but that instead every child is capable of becoming an accomplished violinist and musician. Dr Suzuki believes that talent is a matter of training – and training from as early an age as possible. (A little later you'll actually hear some of our 5- and 6-year-olds playing for you. I think you'll be more than a little surprised.)

It dawned on Dr Suzuki many years ago that children everywhere learn to speak by the most natural and instinctive of methods – namely by listening to others, listening to the same words and expressions over and over again, all day, every day, from birth, until they begin to acquire and use the language themselves. He reasoned that by applying this natural 'learning method' to other subjects, any child's potential could be developed to a high standard of ability. And he began by applying it to learning to play the violin, an instrument at which he himself is a master.

But enough of the 'history' lesson. You want to know what we do. Very young children begin by joining in games in which they're given toy violins and sticks for bows. What is important here is that they learn the correct violin-playing posture and are also taught the basic etiquette of the stage. They then continue, both in group and individual sessions, to play simple pieces by constantly listening and repeating. A word of warning for you all, children and parents. You can't go into this half-heartedly, I'm afraid. We are absolutely convinced that Dr Suzuki's method works and that children acquire immense enjoyment out of learning to play, but they must persevere at all times, and you parents must do all you can to help.

I feel that I've said enough for the moment, so I'll pause to allow you to ask me any questions you may have about what I've said so far.

TUTOR:	Now rewind the tape, listen again and check your answers.
TUTOR:	Part 2. Questions 11–24. You're going to hear a radio interview and will have to fill in the missing information in the table. But first, study the table.*
	Now listen to the interview and fill in or write down the missing information. Ready?
INTERVIEWER:	Today, the third in our weekly series of programmes under the title 'Society', we're going to look at leisure activities in Great Britain, and our first guest is Jane White, a journalist. Jane, welcome to the programme.
JANE:	Thank you. It's nice to be here.
INTER.:	Now, perhaps what we ought to do first is to look at some facts and figures, which I know you have with you, and then to discuss some of the implications of those figures.
JANE:	Fine. Yes.
INTER.:	Then we'll bring in some of our other guests. So, first of all, what are the most popular leisure activities that we indulge in?
JANE:	Well, I'm taking my information from a survey carried out in 1977. Well, I know it seems some time ago, but I think that although some forms of leisure activity have increased in popularity since then, the figures are still pretty representative. Firstly, surveys like this divide pastimes into three: home-based activities, sporting activities, and other leisure activities.
INTER.:	And of the home-based activities, *is* watching television the most popular activity – as I suspect?
JANE:	Yes, it is – or at least it was, with a massive 98% men *and* women watching at least once in a four-week period.
INTER.:	Do you think that figure might have decreased now?
JANE:	It's possible, but er well of course just as many now probably watch video films on their television set, and won't be counted in any television programme-watching survey.
INTER.:	What else do we do?
JANE:	Well, not surprisingly perhaps, listening to the radio comes next in popularity to television. Interestingly, and this is quite obviously very *English*, 50% of men in full-time employment do gardening.
INTER.:	I'm obviously very un-English. I never go near my garden! But I have hobbies at home. Are hobbies not very popular?
JANE:	No, and I found this quite surprising. Only 13% of men in full-time employment do some hobby at home, and the figure's even smaller for others: only 8%. And what's more interesting is that apparently only 3% of *all* women do some kind of hobby at home.
INTER.:	Yes, you would have thought that a lot of women did knitting, or played the piano and so on, wouldn't you? Perhaps the survey didn't allow for some of these. I don't know.
JANE:	No, maybe not.

INTER.:	However, what about sports?
JANE:	Well, again, few surprises, I think. Outdoor sports are the most popular with 52% of men in full-time employment taking part in some outdoor sport or other.
INTER.:	What about other men?
JANE:	The figure is lower there: only 35%.
INTER.:	Over 15% lower, in fact. – Now, you've used the phrase 'men in full-time employment' a number of times. How significant is this when talking about leisure?
JANE:	Well, it's an economic thing. While many of the others may only be in part-time employment or be unemployed, and therefore have more leisure time to fill, it's often a question of money. You see, 38% of men in full-time employment do some sort of indoor sport compared with only 12% of other men. You've got to remember that a lot of indoor games – badminton and so on – cost money: kit, hiring the court, and so forth . . .
INTER.:	Yes, I can see that. But to finish this part, you said there was a third category of leisure activities.
JANE:	Yes, just those activities other than home-based or sports.
INTER.:	And the most popular there is . . . ?
JANE:	Oh, by a long way, going out for a meal or a drink.
INTER.:	And is there this sort of difference again? I mean, the difference we were talking about a moment ago?
JANE:	Certainly. Whereas for those in full-time employment the figures are 78% men and 74% women, the figures for others are 53% men and 51% women.
INTER.:	I suppose the difference is probably men going out for a drink alone or with their mates?
JANE:	I don't know, but I suspect so. Oh, by the way, I also suspect that the figures (men and women) might be closer now than when this survey was done.
INTER.:	Just one last question. Did anything surprise you about these last figures?
JANE:	Well, yes, and it also saddened me. The number of people going on 'Visits to the countryside' was surprisingly low, I thought. Only 8–10% of all people saying that they went on a visit to the countryside. It's a shame, don't you think, when we have such beautiful countryside in Britain?
INTER.:	Yes, I do. But perhaps our next guest will add his comments to those we've already made . . .
TUTOR:	Now rewind the tape, listen again and check your answers.

Coursebook pp 106–107

Classroom treatment

1 Students cover the answers and Explanations of answers for Part 3.
2 Students do the test.
3 Students compare and discuss their answers.
4 Students read the answers and Explanations of answers.

🖭 Tapescript

TUTOR:	Part 3. Questions 25–29. Read the five multiple-choice items carefully and then listen to a telephone conversation between a man and a woman. But first read the items.★
	Now listen and answer the multiple-choice items. Ready?

MR JAMES:	Fernside Tennis Club. Can I help you?
MRS SKINNER:	Yes, I'd like to speak to Mr James, please.
MR JAMES:	Speaking. What can I do for you?
MRS SKINNER:	My name's Mrs Skinner and I wrote to you over a week ago . . .
MR JAMES:	Ah, yes . . . Yes, I remember, Mrs Skinner. It was about the fact that you'll have to drop out of the evening classes, wasn't it?
MRS SKINNER:	Yes, but . . .
MR JAMES:	How is your leg, by the way?
MRS SKINNER:	Well, it's kind of you to ask. I'm hobbling around on crutches, but managing all right . . .
MR JAMES:	Oh, good.
MRS SKINNER:	However, I'm really ringing up to find out if you got my letter and what you're going to do about the situation. As I said, I'd only had one lesson before I had my accident – you know I broke my leg – so obviously I feel that I'm entitled to some of my money back . . .
MR JAMES:	Are you suggesting that the Club is somehow responsible for your . . .?
MRS SKINNER:	No, I'm not suggesting that at all . . .
MR JAMES:	Well, it certainly sounds like it to me.
MRS SKINNER:	No, you know full well, as I explained in my letter, that I broke my leg when I fell down some steps at home . . .
MR JAMES:	But didn't you enjoy the lessons?
MRS SKINNER:	Well, I enjoyed the *lesson* and I think tennis is a super game. But that's beside the point. The point is – or points are that firstly you haven't replied to my letter, and secondly that I feel your Club should refund some of the fees I paid. After all, we were asked to pay the whole fees on the first night – £30 – which I did.
MR JAMES:	And then you had this accident.
MRS SKINNER:	Yes. Which quite clearly means that I've had to drop out of the course.
MR JAMES:	But when you paid for the course, Mrs Skinner, you paid for a series of fifteen tennis lessons with professional coaching . . .
MRS SKINNER:	Yes, I'm not arguing about that. And the coach was excellent.
MR JAMES:	But the point I want to make is that we can't refund any of your fees, whatever the reason.
MRS SKINNER:	Not even in the case of someone who . . .
MR JAMES:	Please, Mrs Skinner. We state quite categorically in our brochure, and you have a copy of it, that fees, once paid, are non-refundable.
MRS SKINNER:	Oh, thank you very much! In other words, if I hadn't been so keen to pay on that first night, you wouldn't now be able to ask me for the fees for the course, since I've dropped out?
MR JAMES:	Well, no, it's not quite that simple. In the first place, you would certainly owe us for that lesson . . .
MRS SKINNER:	That I agree with.
MR JAMES:	. . . *and* you would still owe us the 'entrance' fee of £5. But that's not the situation now, and I'm afraid there's nothing else I can do.
MRS SKINNER:	Well, in that case, I'm afraid I shall have to consult a solicitor.
MR JAMES:	You do as you think fit, Mrs Skinner, but I feel a solicitor will advise you not to pursue this matter any further.
MRS SKINNER:	Well, I certainly shan't leave it there. Thank you for your time. Goodbye.
TUTOR:	Now rewind the tape, listen again and check your answers.
	And that's the end of Unit 14.

Exam advice **Classroom treatment** Before reading the Ten Golden Rules over with the students, see how many of the rules the students can already suggest themselves.

UNIT 15 Aspects of Education

PAPER 5: **INTERVIEW**

Aims of the Unit
1 To familiarise students further with the style of questions and photos that appear in the Interview Paper.
2 To provide further practice in dealing with passages.
3 To familiarise students with the content, language and procedures connected with the third part of the Interview Paper, i.e. topics, discussions, role play, etc.
4 To provide students with practical tips and advice on how to tackle the Proficiency Interview Paper.
5 To expand students' knowledge of vocabulary connected to the topic of *Aspects of Education*.

Coursebook pp 108–109

Exercise 1 As in previous Units, this should be regarded as a warm-up phase and should therefore not take up too much time. Students will appreciate however that this is a topic which is likely to come up in the Proficiency Interview and that this discussion phase could provide them with valuable practice.

Exercise 2 Follow the procedures suggested for similar activities in Units 5 and 10 of the Coursebook.

Dealing with passages

Suggested Answers

Passage a): (Slightly) formal, probably written language, possibly an extract from a book or article. *Comment and discussion:* opinions on the three distinctive features of the British educational system; describing the school system in own country; discussing the ideal school system.

Passage b): Neutral/informal language, very probably spoken language (use of short forms *don't*, *what's*), and probably spoken by a student during conversation with friends/relatives. *Comment and discussion:* opinions on what the student said; explaining why students might feel like this; discussing how this kind of attitude can be overcome or avoided.

Passage c): Formal, written language, probably an extract from a newspaper article or from a letter to a serious newspaper. *Comment and discussion:* talking about one's own experience of CALL; discussing the value of computers in learning and whether they can or should replace the teacher.

Coursebook pp 110–111

Preparing for the third phase of the Interview

The third part of the Interview is described by the Cambridge Examinations Syndicate as a 'Structured Communication Exercise.' This term can cover a wide range of activities such as those mentioned on page 110 of the Coursebook. What all these activities have in common is that they aim to involve candidates in an exchange of information or opinion with one another or with the examiner. In some of the activities the candidate may be presented with material (text or illustration) to study before talking, in others they may simply be asked to talk. Pages 110, 111 and 133 present six different kinds of structured communication exercise. It is important that students should realise the variety of tasks they may meet in this part of the Interview and also have practice in all of them.

The Cambridge Examinations Syndicate sends local examination centres a variety of materials for the oral examiner to use in the third part of the Interview, some of which involve one-to-one interviews with the examiner and others which involve group interviews. Again, students should be prepared to handle either kind of interview situation. Exercises **1–4** on pages 110–111 could provide material for either one-to-one or group interviews, whereas Exercise **5** on page 111 is specifically a group interview.

N.B. Candidates may or may not be given time to make notes in the examination.

Classroom treatment As it is a good idea for all students to gain experience in all these kinds of activities, we suggest you spread the preparation for this third part of the Paper over two lessons, concentrating in the first lesson on Exercises **1–3** and in the second on Exercises **4** and **5**.

Exercise 1
1 Ask each student to make notes on the first topic i.e. 'Memories of my early education'.
2 Ask 2 or 3 students to speak in turn to the class as a whole on this topic.
3 Divide students into groups of four and give them each one of the remaining topics to prepare and make notes on.
4 Each student in each group talks to the others in his group about his ideas on the topic received. The others listen, interrupt, enquire, ask for clarification or exemplification, etc. as they see fit.

Exercise 2 As suggested in the Coursebook, with one student taking on the role of candidate and the other that of examiner. Students can then change roles and possibly discuss other topics e.g. Living in the town v. living in the country; Drugs; Is a job necessary? etc.

Exercise 3 As suggested in the Coursebook and for Exercise **2**. Other practice headlines (not thematically related) might be: 'Footballer in tug-of-war'; 'Embryo inherits £1 billion'; 'Dog – the hero of the day'.

Exercise 4 Students can do this in pairs.

Exercise 5 Students are often wary of role play. This reticence can be due to two main factors: associating role play with drama or acting; and having difficulty in identifying with the role they are assigned. Both these fears can be legitimately calmed! Firstly, role play as envisaged by the Cambridge Examinations Syndicate does not involve acting, but simply seeing something from a particular person's point of view, and discussing from that point of view, as is sometimes required by composition titles. This kind of task simply requires students to synthesise and express current arguments. The second problem i.e. of lack of identification with an assigned role, comes about to a large extent because students do not fully understand or appreciate the situation or position involved in that role. If, for example, someone were asked to argue off the cuff from a vegetarian's point of view, they might have difficulty, but after three or four minutes preparing their arguments they would find this task much easier. Advise students therefore to do their preparation as carefully as possible. Practice makes perfect in this kind of task as in others.

Classroom treatment

1 Divide the students into groups of four or five. (If necessary, leave out one of the roles to match the number of students in your class.)
2 Students make brief notes on their arguments.
3 Students study the language of argument.
4 Each student in the group takes it in turn briefly to state his point of view.
5 Discussion of the topic with each student arguing from the point of view of his role.
6 Students could then report back to the other groups in the class on what decisions had been reached in their groups.
7 Students could re-group and be assigned different roles to those they'd played in the previous discussion and then the same task could begin again. This would help students see the requirements of role play more clearly.

Coursebook pp 112–114

Exam guidance **Classroom treatment** Follow the procedure suggested in the *Exam guidance* sections of Units 11–14 i.e.
1 Ask students to do this part of the test.
2 Ask students what advice they think they would give anyone for this part of the test.
3 Read through with the students the *Exam advice* given in the Coursebook on this part of the test.

Exercise 2 **Suggested answers**
a) This text is almost certainly spoken English, taken perhaps from a conversation with a friend or colleague. It could of course be from a personal letter.
b) This text is almost certainly written English (note the use, for example, of present participle constructions), and sounds very much as if it might be an extract from a science fiction story.
c) This text is definitely written English, and almost certainly an entry in a general dictionary. It is not technical or scientific enough to be an entry in a medical textbook or dictionary.

Exercise 3a **Classroom treatment** Choose whether to conduct this structured communication exercise as a talk or a discussion depending on individual students' needs and weaknesses.

Exercise 3b **Possible answers** The notes made for each of the roles mentioned in this exercise could be as follows:

A medical researcher: Our task – to find cures for illnesses and diseases. Don't like using animals, but sometimes essential. Question of balancing the life of an animal against the good for thousands of humans. Whenever possible, of course, we experiment on humans, as in Common Cold Centres.

A doctor: I am an animal lover, but I am first and foremost a doctor – concerned with making sick patients well and healthy. I prescribe the best medicines available, and have to accept the fact that some have been developed through experiments on animals. Would still be happier if animals were not used in this way.

Someone who has just benefited from a new drug: This will sound selfish – just been cured from an illness I've had 20 years. So happy! Don't care how it was developed. I think deep down most people would react like me.

An animal rights campaigner: No justification for using animals in research: why make dumb animals suffer needlessly. Science must be able to experiment without using live animals – and if people want cures for illnesses and diseases, people should be prepared to offer themselves as 'guinea pigs'.

A parent: Son/daughter suffers dreadfully from asthma or hayfever – school work suffering, sleepless nights, can't go on public transport, etc. – so would love to find a cure. But would not agree to animals being used in any research to find a cure.

Exam guidance for possible Group Interview

Some candidates or centres may opt for a Group Interview format instead of a one-to-one (Examiner-Candidate) interview. Here are some suggestions for helping students to prepare for this situation:

1 **Talking about the photo and discussing related topics**

Ask students, in groups, to prepare questions about the photo to ask each other. When discussing related topics, make each student in the group responsible for getting other students' opinions and comments on *one* of the general questions or topics.

2 **Commenting on passages**

Ask each student in the group to comment on *one* of the passages for the others. This will involve reporting, summarising, perhaps quoting briefly (though *not* reading the whole passage aloud), and then expressing an opinion on the content.

3 **Discussing a piece of realia**

Where possible, and before a general discussion or role play, make each student in the group responsible for reporting and/or commenting on just *one* part of what is presented (e.g. the sports aspect of a school prospectus, accidents in the home as opposed to road accidents, etc.).

Conducting mock interviews

Mock interviews can be invaluable in reducing students' worries about the interview. How you conduct them will depend to a large extent on the size of your class, but here are two suggestions:

1 Set the rest of the class reading or written work to do while you interview the students one by one. This can be done over two or·three lessons.

2 Let students interview each other in pairs while a third student listens and gives marks.

In either case, of course, you could record the interviews. These can then be marked later either just by you or through class discussion. If the latter procedure is adopted, *all* students' performances must be discussed, not just one or two. If there is likely to be any student resistance to such a procedure, then recordings can usefully be listened to and discussed with individual students.

Proficiency
Practice Exam
Information

Introduction

The Proficiency Practice Exam contains five complete Papers. Each Paper is equivalent to a full Cambridge Proficiency Paper in level, form and length.

The Exam can be used as either

1 further classroom (or homework) practice material in preparation for the Proficiency Exam towards the end of or on completion of the course; or
2 material to be administered as a 'mock' or practice examination on completion of the course, and marked accordingly.

If the Papers are set as 'mock' examination Papers, it is important that they be administered and timed as near to examination conditions as possible so that prospective candidates become accustomed to the idea of having to complete Papers within the set time allowed.

IMPORTANT: In some parts of the Practice Exam, the sample of language on which Papers are based is that taught in the Coursebook. If they are marked as 'mock' examinations, therefore, while success may give an indication of high achievement in the course, such results should not be taken to be an indication of the same degree of success in the Proficiency proper.

Any attempt to assess or forecast individual students' possible success (or failure) in the Proficiency examination from results in this Exam should be made with extreme caution.

Coverage and times allowed

The Practice Exam contains the following:

		Time allowed in minutes
Paper 1:	Reading Comprehension	60
Paper 2:	Composition	120
Paper 3:	Use of English	120
Paper 4:	Listening Comprehension	25 approx.
Paper 5:	Interview	15 approx.
Total:		340 approx.

General method of administration

Papers 1, 2 and 3 (Reading Comprehension, Composition and Use of English) should be administered in the same way as all the end-of-Unit tests in the Coursebook. As throughout the course, students should be advised again to read all instructions carefully, read items or texts through completely before answering questions, write clearly and make sure that they complete the Paper in the time given.

For each 'text' in Paper 4 Listening Comprehension, the following procedure is recommended:

1 Before playing the recording of the first text, give students a minute in which to study the items, read an incomplete form, or whatever.

2 After the minute, tell the students that you are going to play the text straight through. During this first listening, they can begin to answer the questions.
3 After the first listening, give them another minute in which to check what they have done.
4 Then play the text for a second time, so that they can finish answering the questions or check what they did when they listened the first time.

IMPORTANT NOTE

The recordings of the Listening Comprehension Paper 4 material include all repetitions, so you will not need to run the cassette back. Please note that when you hear a BLEEP, this indicates where you will need to pause the tape to give students time to read the questions.

All you need do for the Listening Comprehension Paper is to instruct students to look at pages 128–131 of the Coursebook; to make sure they have pens or pencils and paper; to read the instructions (for the Paper) with them; to switch on the cassette player at the beginning of the recording and to let it run, except for pausing it when you hear a BLEEP.

Although the Paper 5 Oral Interview material provided at the end of the Exam is probably best used as classroom practice material (in the same way as the material provided in the Coursebook), it can of course also be used as 'mock' interview material by those teachers who find that they can devote 5–10 minutes to individual students at the end of the course. If time can be found, students find such an interview invaluable preparation for the real thing. The procedure will be very much as classroom preparation using such material. (See this TG page 115.)

You will notice that there are three activities proposed on page 133 for the third part of the Interview Paper. In the Proficiency Examination the oral examiner also has a range of activities to choose from for each candidate (as explained on page 113 of the TG). Select from and order these activities as you think best in terms of exam security and exposing different students to different activities.

You will also notice that the activities proposed on page 133 involve group interviews. The Cambridge Examination Syndicate provides examination centres with materials for both one-to-one and group interviews, so students should be trained to handle both kinds of interview. (See this TG page 115.)

You could adapt the group activities on page 133 to one-to-one interviews by turning Exercises 3a) and 3b) into discussions on 'The increase in crime' and 'Animal rights' respectively, and in Exercise 4 by simply asking a student to read the newspaper article and then to comment on it.

No scoring procedure has been provided for Paper 5 Oral Interview since it is felt that the emphasis here should be more on encouragement for individual students than on giving grades or assessments.

One final note. While students may write their answers to certain Papers on the Practice Exam pages (as they will do in the Proficiency proper), they will have to be provided with ordinary writing paper for the Composition and Use of English Papers (and perhaps for certain other Papers at the teacher's discretion). At the end of a 'mock' exam Paper, test papers should be taken in and marked as quickly as possible in order to ensure the speediest feedback for students.

N.B. In the Proficiency Exam students are given an Answer Sheet for Paper 1. They write on paper provided by the Examination Centre for Paper 2. And for Papers 3 and 4 they record their answers on the question paper.

Detailed answers and marking schemes

Paper 1: Reading Comprehension
Coursebook pp 116–121

Answer key

SECTION A

1 C; 2 B; 3 C; 4 D; 5 A; 6 C; 7 D;
8 A; 9 D; 10 B; 11 A; 12 C; 13 A;
14 A; 15 B; 16 B; 17 B; 18 C; 19 B;
20 D; 21 B; 22 C; 23 A; 24 A; 25 C

SECTION B

First passage: 26 C; 27 D; 28 D; 29 D;
                  30 D; 31 A
Second passage: 32 A; 33 B; 34 B; 35 C
Third passage: 36 C; 37 B; 38 D; 39 C;
                  40 D

Suggested marking scheme

SECTION A

25 items, 1 mark for each correct answer   25

SECTION B

15 items, 2 marks for each correct answer   30
                                                 —
Possible maximum total for the whole paper: 55
                                                 —

Paper 2: Composition
Coursebook p 122

Suggested marking scheme

Use an impression mark to assess the compositions
(each out of a possible total of 20), taking the
following factors into account:
– the quality of the language employed
– the range and appropriateness of vocabulary and
  sentence structure
– the correctness of grammar, punctuation and
  spelling
– the naturalness and appropriateness of language
– the relevance and organisation of the compositions
– length requirements

N.B. the length requirements which are given beside
each composition title are flexible.

The University of Cambridge Local Examinations
Syndicate has published the following table to show
how the impression mark is given at Proficiency level:

18–20	Excellent	Error-free, substantial and varied material, resourceful and controlled in language and expression.
16–17	Very Good	Good realisation of task, ambitious and natural in style.
12–15	Good	Sufficient assurance and freedom from basic error to maintain theme.
8–11	Pass	Clear realisation of task, reasonably correct and natural.
5–7	Weak	Near to pass level in general scope, but with either numerous errors or too elementary or translated in style.
0–4	Very Poor	Basic errors, narrowness of vocabulary.

The Syndicate interprets these marks as follows:

40% of the total (i.e. 8 out of 20)	– rough pass level
60%	– good pass
75%–90%	– a very good standard

Paper 3: Use of English
Coursebook pp 123–127

Answer key

SECTION A

1 1 as; 2 for; 3 did; 4 from/about; 5 at; 6 but; 7 some;
   8 on; 9 with; 10 what; 11 at; 12 there; 13 had;
   14 for; 15 as; 16 in/through/throughout; 17 but;
   18 of; 19 had; 20 such

2 a) In spite of the weather/weather's not being/In spite of the fact that the weather wasn't very promising, we still went to the beach.
   b) Her accident stopped/prevented her (from) riding for six months.
   c) On hearing the news, she broke down.
   d) No sooner had I left the house than I heard the phone ring.
   e) Strong as/though he is/may be, he still can't lift that box.
   f) He must have been having a bath when I called.
   g) I'd rather you didn't ask her to the party.
   h) There isn't a more dedicated singer than John in the choir/in the choir than John.

3 a) she/he/I/they/you/we had gone/stayed
   b) ought to/should have had/got
   c) (first) met him/was (first) introduced to him
   d) I think so/I do/I think we should
   e) would have done/solved/approached it; did it
   f) The more

4 a) The concert didn't come up to/meet our expectations.
   b) His advice to me was to rest for a month/that I should/ought to rest for a month.
   c) He managed to get the job finished thanks to his secretary's efficiency.
   OR Thanks to his secretary's efficiency he managed to get the job finished.
   d) After the book, the film was terribly disappointing.
   e) Somehow he had his hand crushed in the car door.
   f) He is practically blind without glasses.
   g) I'd rather you didn't go/weren't going on that trip.
   h) She is believed to have been born in Australia.

SECTION B

Answers to questions a)-n) may well be worded differently to the following suggested answers, but the information and ideas they contain should be the same.

a) To give the idea that there are many treasure-hunters, that they operate where they don't belong and that they are aggressive.
b) That of an army leaving its camp.
c) The number of treasure-hunters is rapidly increasing.
d) Initially to report on metal-detectors and archaeology, and in the longer term to try and legislate on the activities of treasure-hunters.
e) 'whose activities are far from being purely negative' and 'they put forward two technical arguments which seem relevant'.

f) To investigate the use of metal-detectors in archaeology.
g) Places which are on an official list that acknowledges that they are of archaeological value.
h) Because they keep for themselves parts of a heritage that belongs to everyone.
i) This refers to the fact that archaeological findings can be made very close to or even on the surface of the earth.
j) They would lack numbers to do all the work required if treasure-hunters handed their finds over to them.
k) If it hadn't been for them.
l) They argue noisily or loudly.
m) They claim to be less interested in making money than in archaeology.
n) Because they are the only people who have definite permission to hunt for archaeological remains.
o) The arguments by treasure-hunters in defence of their activities:

   – Their right to exercise a healthy and non-violent activity.
   – The importance of certain discoveries they have made.
   – The fact that official archaeologists also sometimes use metal-detectors.
   – That they are not motivated mainly by financial gain.
   – That archaeology shouldn't be reserved for official archaeologists.
   – That they record isolated finds.
   – That they save metal objects from destruction.

Suggested marking scheme

SECTION A

1: 20 items, 1 mark each		20
2: 8 sentences, 2 marks each		16
3: 6 sentences, 2 marks each		12
4: 8 sentences, 2 marks each		16
Possible total maximum:		64

SECTION B

14 questions (questions a-n), 3 marks each	42
Summary (question o)	24
Possible total maximum:	66
Possible maximum total for the whole Paper:	130

Allotment of marks

In Section A **2, 3, 4** award half marks for partially correct sentences.

In Section B questions (a)-(n), answers should be coherent, relevant and in correct English. Award half marks where appropriate.

In Section B question (o), the summary should be well-expressed and contain all and only the relevant information. Allot marks accordingly.

Paper 4: Listening Comprehension

Tapescript 🔲

FIRST PART

TUTOR: Practice Exam. Paper 4: Listening Comprehension. Look at page 128. For the first part of the test, Questions 1–10, you'll hear a telephone conversation in which a person enquires about courses at a secretarial college. Read the instructions and questions carefully. You'll hear the conversation twice.
(PAUSE)
Now listen and fill in or tick the required information. Ready?

MARY: (*dialling*) Three, five, three, seven, six, two, four, one.
(*under her breath*) Oh, come on. (*pause*) Ah, good.

RECEPTION-
IST: Good afternoon. 'All-Office' Secretarial College. Can I help you?

MARY: Er, yes. I saw your ad in yesterday's paper, and I'd like to know more about the courses you run.

R.: Of course. I could send you a brochure, if you like. Or I could tell you a little about the courses now.

MARY: Well, I'd like to know a little now if I may.

R.: Perhaps first of all I should say that most of the courses we run include typing, shorthand and general office procedures. Is that the kind of course you wanted, or did you want word processing and computer studies as well?

MARY: No, just an ordinary course to start with. I'm a complete beginner – I can't type or anything, and somebody told me I'd have to learn to type before I could do anything with word processors anyway.

R.: Yes, that's right. Well, what would you like to know?

MARY: Well, when does the next 'general office' course start?

R.: The next one. Let me see . . . We're in week 10 of the present one. Um . . . ah, here it is, Monday, 16th May.

MARY: May 16th.

R.: Yes. And it lasts 12 weeks. So that means you'd start on May 16th and finish on Friday, 5th August.

MARY: 5th August. And I presume you have a half-term, do you?

R.: Yes. I don't know the dates exactly. But you'd get that information later.

MARY: Yes, I see. Um-How many hours do you have a day?

R.: Well, generally you have three hours in the morning, 9 to 12, and then two hours in the afternoon. That's five hours a day, five days a week.

MARY: And how much does the course cost?

R.: £400. But you may be able to get a government grant to help you.

MARY: £400 did you say?

R.: Yes. But as I said, you might be able to get a government grant – and you can pay in instalments anyway.

MARY: Oh, good. By the way, just out of interest, are all the students girls?

R.: Not all, but about 90%. We get some male students with us who want to go into computers, so they take a course with us. They find the general office procedure useful as well.

MARY: It sounds as if it's just what I need. But I live in the country, and it would be best if I could get accommodation in town. Can you help with accommodation?

R.: Well, we're not a residential college, but we can try to find you a room with a family.

MARY: I've never lived away from home before. Could you give me an idea of the prices?

R.: Roughly speaking, a room with just bed and breakfast would be about £15–£20 a week. But if you wanted an evening meal as well every day, it would be about £25 a week.

MARY: Oh . . . I don't know. I'll have to think about it.

R.: Well, I'll send you a brochure and then you can fill in an application form if you think you'd like to come.

MARY: Yes, could you do that?

R.: Of course. If you let me have your name and address, I'll get it in the post to you today. But don't forget that term starts in two weeks' time, so you'll have to make up your mind fairly quickly. Oh, I should have said: if you want to come in and see us, come in any time.

MARY: Thank you. I might do that.

R.: Well, now, can I have your name, please?

MARY: Yes, it's Mary Mills. And my address is . . .

TUTOR: Now listen to the conversation again and check your answers. Ready?

(*Conversation repeated on tape*)

TUTOR: That's the end of the first part of the test.

SECOND PART

TUTOR: Second part. Look at page 129. You'll hear part of a radio programme. Read the instructions and questions carefully. For each of the questions 11–16, you'll be asked to tick one of the boxes – A, B, C or D. You'll hear the piece twice.
(PAUSE)
Now listen and answer the questions. Ready?

ANNOUNCER: It's just coming up to eight o'clock, and time for this week's edition of 'Ask The Panel', the programme in which you the listeners can quiz a panel of distinguished guests on their views of issues of the day. And here's your host, Daniel James.

DANIEL: Good evening and welcome again to 'Ask The Panel'. And this week we've come to Hightown Polytechnic. Our team consists of the Right Honourable James Smith, Member of Parliament for Hightown. Perhaps unusually for MPs nowadays, Mr Smith was actually born and brought up in this area. We are also pleased to welcome Mrs Joan Hunter, who is a housewife and an active member of both the Human Rights and Animal Rights movements. On my right is Mr Jeremy Slade, best known to many of you as the lead guitarist in the 'Blue Monday' pop group. He was born and raised in Hightown, and has recently become

concerned about the welfare of the town and has just been elected to the town council. And the last member of the panel is Claire Cook, journalist and agony column writer for the 'Daily News'. With the introductions over, may we have our first question, please, from Ms Stella Johnson?

STELLA: In view of recent legislation allowing even larger transport vehicles (namely 'juggernauts') to travel the roads of this country, what are the panel's views on the subject, bearing in mind that many old buildings are already beginning to suffer badly from traffic vibration?

DANIEL: Thank you, Ms Johnson. 'In view of recent legislation allowing even larger transport vehicles ("juggernauts") to travel the roads of this country,' Ms Johnson asks for the panel's views on the subject, bearing in mind, she says, that many old buildings are already beginning to suffer badly from traffic vibration.' James Smith?

JAMES: Well, it's quite clear to me that Ms Johnson is as concerned as I am about the most recent legislation which has increased the maximum size for transport vehicles in this country. Now while I am in sympathy with goods haulage firms who wish to carry as much as they can by road as cheaply as possible – that is with large juggernaut lorries, often with massive trailers – they *cannot* be allowed to travel through many of our smaller towns which were just not designed for large amounts of heavy through-traffic. I would like to say that I personally voted against this proposal in parliament and shall continue to fight to have the legislation revoked – or at least amended. Let us by all means have these massive vehicles on our motorways: after all, they have been designed to take heavy loads. But we must fight to preserve our history, our heritage and the peace and quiet of many small towns and villages. And one thing we can do is to ban these juggernauts from roads other than motorways.

DANIEL: Thank you, James. Joan Hunter.

JOAN: It's terribly sad, you know, but thousands of animals are killed on our roads every year. You only have to drive on a motorway or along country roads early in the morning particularly: they're often littered with animal corpses. And before anyone wonders why I've mentioned animals first, it's because I'm concerned with all life – animal and human. Yes, thousands of people are killed or injured on our roads every year, too. What I am saying is that motor vehicles and the roads they need to drive on are killers. I can't ask to turn the clock back: we can't *not* have motor vehicles and roads now. They're with us to stay. But we can control the speeds at which vehicles have to travel, and we can (and *must*) control the size of vehicles.

DANIEL: Jeremy?

JEREMY: There was a time when I used to travel round Europe with my own group, with all our stage sets and so on, in what you'd call a juggernaut. I often wondered what the residents in small German or Italian towns thought when we rolled up in this massive thing. Now I know, and I wish I'd known then what our 'transport' was doing to their history. We've got some old buildings here in Hightown which must be three or four hundred years old. Some of them are beginning to crack very badly and show other signs of wear – just from town traffic. I mean, from the rumble and vibration of the everyday traffic in the town. Now, God knows what would happen to them if juggernauts came lumbering through the town. It's not only old buildings either. Just about everything and everybody suffers when these things pass. The ones they're proposing to allow on our roads are about the size of an ordinary house, and the noise is deafening. Since I'm now a local councillor, I for one will be prepared to lie in the road to stop one going through here!

DANIEL: And Claire Cook?

CLAIRE: What can I add? – I agree with the rest of the panel whole-heartedly – except to say that these juggernauts will add yet more pollution to our already polluted air. I'd probably regret it if it ever happened, but I

often pray for the day petrol runs out and there are no cars, buses, or lorries on the road at all. I think that we'd finally all begin to breathe fresh air again, and many of us would start getting some valuable exercise – either through walking or cycling.

DANIEL: Thank you, panel, for your views. We'll leave on that refreshing note . . .

TUTOR: Now listen again and check your answers. Ready?

(*Radio programme repeated on tape.*)

TUTOR: That's the end of the second part of the test.

THIRD PART

TUTOR: Third part. Look at pages 130–131. You'll hear part of a radio 'Book at Bedtime' story.
Read the instructions and questions carefully. For each of the questions 17–22, you'll be asked to tick one of the boxes – A, B, C or D. You'll hear the extract twice.
(PAUSE)
Now listen and answer the questions. Ready?

ANNOUNCER: The time is now 10.30, and time for our 'Book at Bedtime', which tonight is a slightly adapted version of H.G. Wells' short story 'The Man Who Could Work Miracles'. It's read by Hugh James.

HUGH: It is doubtful whether the gift was innate. For my own part, I think it came to him suddenly. Indeed, until he was thirty he was a sceptic, and did not believe in miraculous powers. And here, since it is the most convenient place, I must mention that he was a little man, and had brown eyes, very erect red hair, a moustache with ends that he twisted up, and freckles. His name was George McWhirter Fotheringay – not the sort of name by any stretch of the imagination to lead to any expectation of miracles – and he was a clerk at Gomshott's. He was very fond of assertive argument, and it was while he was asserting the impossibility of miracles that he had his first intimation of his extraordinary powers. This particular argument was being held in the bar of the Long

Dragon public house, and Toddy Beamish was conducting the opposition by a monotonous but effective 'So *you* say', that drove Mr Fotheringay to the very limit of his patience.

There were present, besides these two, a very dusty cyclist, landlord Cox, and Miss Maybridge, the perfectly respectable and rather large barmaid of the Dragon. Miss Maybridge was standing with her back to Mr Fotheringay, washing glasses; the others were watching him, more or less amused by the present ineffectiveness of the assertive method. Somewhat annoyed by the tactics of Mr Beamish, Mr Fotheringay determined to make an unusual rhetorical effort. 'Look here, Mr Beamish,' said Mr Fotheringay. 'Let us clearly understand what a miracle is. It's something contrariwise to the course of nature done by power of Will, something that couldn't happen without being specially willed.'

'So *you* say,' said Mr Beamish. Mr Fotheringay appealed to the cyclist, who had until now been a silent listener, and received his agreement – given with a hesitating cough and a glance at Mr Beamish. The landlord would express no opinion, and Mr Fotheringay, returning to Mr Beamish, received the unexpected concession of a qualified assent to his definition of a miracle. 'For instance,' said Mr Fotheringay, greatly encouraged. 'Here would be a miracle. That oil lamp, in the natural course of nature, couldn't burn like that upside-down, could it, Beamish?'

'*You* say it couldn't,' said Beamish.

'And you?' said Fotheringay. 'You don't mean to say – eh?'

'No,' said Beamish reluctantly. 'No, it couldn't.'

'Very well,' said Mr Fotheringay. 'Then here comes someone, as it might be me, along here, and stands as it might be here, and says to the lamp, as I might do, collecting all my will – "Turn upside-down without breaking, and go on burning steadily," and – Hullo!'

It was enough to make anyone say 'Hullo!'. The impossible, the incredible, was visible to them all. The lamp hung inverted in the air, burning quietly with its flame pointing down. It was as solid, as indisputable as ever a lamp was, the common lamp of the Long Dragon bar. Mr Fotheringay stood with an extended forefinger and the knitted brow of one anticipating a catastrophic crash. The cyclist, who was sitting next to the lamp, ducked and jumped across the bar. Everybody jumped, more or less. Miss Maybridge turned and screamed. For nearly three seconds the lamp remained still. A faint cry of mental distress came from Mr Fotheringay. 'I can't keep it up,' he said, 'any longer.' He staggered back, and the inverted lamp suddenly flared, fell against the corner of the bar, bounced aside, smashed upon the floor, and went out.

TUTOR: Now listen again and check your answers. Ready?

('*Book at Bedtime*' repeated on tape.)

TUTOR: And that's the end of the test.

Answer key

FIRST PART
1 Monday, 16th May; 2 12 weeks; 3 May 16th to Friday, 5th August; 4 5; 5 Yes; 6 £400; 7 Yes; 8 with a family; 9 £15–£20 per week; 10 £25 per week

SECOND PART
11 C; 12 B; 13 A; 14 B; 15 D; 16 D

THIRD PART
17 A; 18 C; 19 D; 20 A; 21 D; 22 D

Suggested marking scheme

22 items, 1 mark each   22
                                                                   ———

Possible total maximum for the whole Paper: 22
                                                                   ———